# HOME BY ANOTHER ROUTE

# HOME
## BY ANOTHER ROUTE

≽ ¥ ≼

## A JOURNAL OF
## ART, MUSIC, AND FAITH

## CHARLES SCRIBNER III

Paulist Press
New York / Mahwah, NJ

Cover image: The Journey of the Magi by Sassetta (Stefano di Giovanni)
Cover design by Dawn Massa, Lightly Salted Graphics
Book design by Lynn Else

Library of Congress Cataloging-in-Publication Data

Names: Scribner, Charles, 1951– author.
Title: Home by another route : a journal of art, music, and faith / Charles Scribner III.
Description: Mahwah, New Jersey : Paulist Press, 2016.
Identifiers: LCCN 2016022451 (print) | LCCN 2016031752 (ebook) | ISBN 9780809153046 (pbk. : alk. paper) | ISBN 9781587686412 (Ebook)
Subjects: LCSH: Scribner, Charles, 1951– | Catholic converts—United States—Biography. | Church year meditations.
Classification: LCC BX4668.S37 A3 2016 (print) | LCC BX4668.S37 (ebook) | DDC 282.092 [B] —dc23
LC record available at https://lccn.loc.gov/2016022451

ISBN 978-0-8091-5304-6 (paperback)
ISBN 978-1-58768-641-2 (e-book)

Published by Paulist Press
997 Macarthur Boulevard
Mahwah, New Jersey 07430

www.paulistpress.com

Printed and bound in the
United States of America

In memory of my mother,
Joan Sunderland Scribner

# Acknowledgments

To Michelle Rapkin, friend and editorial colleague of three decades, I owe heartfelt thanks for her painstaking—yet painless—pruning of my original journal into a publishable book. Trace Murphy, Editorial Director of Paulist Press, provided the encouragement, insight, and expertise that guided both book and author along the happy route to publication. To Trace and all his talented colleagues at Paulist Press I am most grateful—onward.

# CONTENTS

When I finished my spiritual journal The Shadow of God on Epiphany, I was tempted to keep going, but I resisted—perhaps as much from laziness as in view of the uncertain path ahead. Looking back with wistfulness, I now wonder, Is this what the Magi experienced after they departed from the warmth and glow of the manger and began their long journey "home by another route," as the angel had instructed them in a dream?

# EPIPHANY

I love the Feast of the Epiphany—and the expectation leading up to it, the perfect antidote to the post-Christmas letdown. On vacation in Florida, a place from which I am always ready to go home—by any route—I felt cheated that in America, the Catholic Church ignores both centuries of tradition and the rest of the Christian world by rushing into the Epiphany the first Sunday of the New Year. I went to Mass and listened to the inspired story of the Three Wise Men from St. Matthew's Gospel and sang heartily "We Three Kings," but with a conviction that this was only a *proleptic* celebration, an anticipation of the Real Feast following Twelfth Night, on the sixth of January.

I was relieved to see that the Park Avenue trees were still lit as I wended my way north to St. Vincent Ferrer for evening Mass. Our secular city still keeps the ancient date of this feast. The evergreens inside the church never glowed more refreshingly, bedecked in their jewels of white lights. The priest, in his homily about the Word—both the word of God and the Word that *is* God, "in the beginning," as St. John's Gospel proclaims—reminded us all that there is nothing abstract about that Word. It is not something that hovers "out there." It is very precise and concrete: it must be spoken and heard (or written and read) to be received and digested—or rejected. At that moment, I knew why I had felt so long in exile. The act of struggling to find words, whether in the mind's ear or on a laptop keyboard, is what gives shape to memories and those fleeting moments of grace that vanish by the light of the next day. I want to preserve this Epiphany beyond the five minutes that remain of it. At the same time, I pray it may light the way home in the days and months to come before the next appearance of the Star. I don't think of this journal as a prayer journal. But perhaps searching for words may yet lead me to the Word.

I have arrived at a quaint, redbrick motel in Pennsylvania Dutch country, with less than half an hour until midnight. This is the farthest west I have ever driven in my life. I have my younger son to thank for this venture, as I am here to pick him up tomorrow and drive him back to school for the beginning of winter term. I thought of both the Magi and my wise father as I drove through the freezing rain in the dark and passed two signs for Bethlehem, the first in New Jersey, the second across the border in Pennsylvania, once famous for steel mills of a bygone era. Then seeing the signs for Emmaus finally rooted Route 78 in the Holy Land.

My father used to tease us that the secret to a happy marriage was to avoid the temptation to take "a new route" when driving with one's wife. The inevitable consequence of getting lost along the way would be an instant source of marital strife. "No new routes" was the slogan he shared with his closest friends at his twenty-fifth wedding anniversary dinner and then reprised five years later at Ritchie's bridal dinner, the evening before our own wedding, twenty-five years ago.

On the solo drive home, I was able to visit the Bruce Museum in Greenwich to see the exhibition of Rubens oil sketches. The centerpieces of the show were a series of oil sketches for Rubens's "Triumph of the Eucharist," the very subject I was studying for my first public lecture (and later dissertation) thirty years ago to the month. Several of them I had never seen before, in the flesh, until today. It was a short detour, but it took me to another home—and back a generation—to where I spent so many happy hours of youth. When I finally reached New York and got to Mass, I learned that today's feast, our Lord's Baptism, was celebrated by the early Church as the original Epiphany. At dusk it capped a series of epiphanies, all reflecting the same Light.

My one regret during yesterday's motor trip accompanied by *Der Rosenkavalier* was that I could not pair my favorite Oktavian—Flicka von Stade—with my definitive Marschallin, Elisabeth Schwarzkopf, who retired from the role she owned years before Flicka sang the part of the young count. To be sure, to have a Marschallin thirty years older than her lover would be stretching more than vocal cords. As if in compensation, I concluded the trip, as I approached the New York skyline, with a CD of Dame Elisabeth's encores. But how I would have loved to hear her sing once again the Marschallin's pensive monologue: "*Die Zeit, die is ein sonderbar Ding….*" Time is indeed a strange and wonderful "creation of the Father who made us all," as today's afternoon mail brought home to me.

I had been dreading this evening's task of taking down the Christmas tree, packing away the ornaments collected along the past twenty-six Christmases Ritchie and I have celebrated together, stripping the tinsel garlands and strings of white lights, and dethroning the angel from her lofty pinnacle, before carting the dry fir tree out the back door. But a large envelope redeemed the day and the beginning of Ordinary Time, as the Church calendar calls these coming weeks between the Epiphany and Lent. It had been forwarded from my old publishing office, which I left six months ago. Postmarked from Austria, it appeared to be a belated Christmas card from some European publisher. I opened the envelope to discover a card with a photograph of a stunningly elegant lady in profile, bowing her head, her right hand lightly supporting it, in deep thought or perhaps prayer. Below was inscribed in gold those thoughts *auf Deutsch*: "*Ein recht glückliches neues Jahr wünscht Ihnen.*" To this formal wish for a truly happy New Year, she added in her own silver script, "Dear Charles,—Your (old) Elisabeth."

I had my Marschallin after all! And then I noticed that the card, which took a month to reach me, had been postmarked the day before Schwarzkopf's eighty-ninth birthday. Her ninetieth will be celebrated, God willing, on December 9th of this new year. Finally, I have a worthy New Year's resolution: to visit her, twenty years since I last saw her in person, at her new home in Schruns, that Austrian ski village where Hemingway, ten years after her birth, completed writing *The Sun Also Rises*. (Does it ever.) And after the sun rises, here I shall call her and try to explain the joy with which this post-Christmas gift was received.

I reached Dame Elisabeth today by phone, but only after waiting an hour for her hairdresser to finish. I had to laugh—it was like the toilette in Act One of *Der Rosenkavalier*. When I finally got through and thanked her for the Christmas photo, she explained that it had been taken during a performance of Strauss's last opera, *Capriccio*, and its pensiveness captured her feeling of advancing age and time. Yet her speaking voice sounded as fresh and unchanged as from her recordings of many decades past. I am reminded of that Roman god Januarius, after whom our first month takes its name. With a double countenance— one old, one young—he looks both backward and forward at the beginning of each new year. I told her that I was determined to come and visit her, and she said she prayed that God ("Someone up there") would keep her alive long enough! He must, I replied. She wants me to send her my article on "The Garden of Love" (from medieval art to Mozart), the subject of my upcoming spring lecture at the Met Museum. "Do you really know about love, too?" she asked. I explained that it was about a theme in art. "Well, send it, why not tomorrow. I know something about art, too." I said I'd follow my father's dictum: "No rush, just do it at once," and, laughing, she said that had been her late husband's—the producer Walter Legge's—philosophy. I'm still trying in vain to find a German translation that captures Dad's wry humor.

The readings at Mass this week are from St. Paul's Epistle to the Hebrews—or so it used to be called. According to Father Baker, scripture scholars no longer believe it was written by St. Paul; it is no longer considered a letter; and the recipients were probably not Hebrew. So what are we left with? Just the message: the poetic image of Christ "higher than the angels" deigning to become, for a time, "lower than the angels" for our sake. Masterpieces need no signatures.

Father Keitz gave as his homily a brief biography of the saint celebrated today, the fourth-century St. Hilary, who was bishop of Poitiers not long after Constantine grafted Christianity onto Imperial Rome. He was married and had children—well prepared, I suppose, to take on the bishop's crook in those early years of battle with paganism and heresies. Perhaps we may yet come full circle.

I am to read from Paul's Letter to the Romans at an annual memorial Mass at St. Jean Baptiste next Thursday. The passage is from chapter 8 and explains our identity as children of God by adoption in the Spirit. It concludes with that powerful image of the universe groaning up to now "as in labor." I could not find a King James edition here, although I am certain there are several in hiding. The first translation I found was the New English Bible—very clear and accurate, but lacking the poetic cadences of earlier versions. More troubling was its repetition of the phrase "sons of God" and its referring to the Spirit as "he." I am not quite ready to reverse millennia of patriarchal language and refer to God and the Spirit both as "She," as Father Greeley often does—to make a very valid point about the limits of our imagination if not our understanding of divinity. Yet I have succumbed to political correctness—at least in the realm of inclusive language.

Then, on a shelf full of art books, I found a paperback of the New American Bible, in which I had inscribed "Lent, 2001." That seems an era ago, an age of pre-9/11 innocence. I had bought my first copy of this authorized Catholic Bible back in 1970, the year I joined the Church as a college student. But this paperback included a new translation of the New Testament published sixteen years later, wherein, thank God, the "three astrologers from the East" have reverted to the "three Magi" of art and legend. No longer is the famous question "Who is my neighbor?" meaninglessly reworded "Who is my fellow man?" in the parable of the good Samaritan; nor is "render unto Caesar the things that are Caesar's" misrendered "what is due Caesar." Even more gratefully, I discovered that St. Paul now describes us as "children of God" and refers to the Spirit as the gender-neutral "it." As tempted as I am to use the magisterial and poetic King James, I shall resist and be thankful for the contemporary resonance of this new version. Paul wrote his original letters, after all, in simple and direct prose. Unlike Molière's *Le bourgeois gentilhomme*, he would not have been delightfully surprised to be told that he had been speaking prose all his life. He knew what he was doing. Poetry will have its day, but for Paul, this prose will do the job. Hemingway once noted, "All you have to do is write one true sentence." Perhaps that should be the touchstone of biblical translation.

I have not spent so much of a Sunday reading in many years. But I could not put down Andrew Greeley's *The Bishop and the Three Kings* and finish the day without a solution to the theft of the Three Kings reliquary from Cologne's cathedral. Father Greeley's inspired—and impish—Bishop Blackie proved a worthy successor to Holmes, as all the pieces fell into place. But in the process, Greeley has left me with an appreciation of still greater mysteries, as enriching as they are insoluble—"arguably," as Blackie would say. The first is Greeley's hallmark theme of God as a pursuing Lover. Midway through the mystery, Blackie urges his nephew

Peter Murphy to pursue his ladylove "like God pursues us, implacably but tenderly." Peter says he is trying but protests that God "doesn't want us the way I want Cindasue."

"Arguably more so."

But Peter counters that "God is probably more restrained" than he is.

"Arguably less."
"That's fascinating theology, Uncle Blackie."
"Merely scripture, properly understood."

I once asked my favorite English novelist (and convert) Graham Greene to write a book about his Catholic faith, his adopted Church, and his theology. He declined and explained—in vintage Greene—that he "preferred that people dug his ideas out of his fiction." Thank God, Greeley is more direct (he is, first and foremost, a priest who preaches through his fiction). So many of his treasures sparkle on the surface: the reader's role is more to reflect than to dig. In one of his several asides to the reader, Bishop Blackie himself reflects on the story of the Magi as reported by St. Matthew and accepted absolutely by Evelyn Waugh's beguiling character Sebastian Flyte (in *Brideshead Revisited*) because it is "a lovely idea." Blackie is more nuanced than Sebastian; he is after all an American bishop, not a carefree English lord. And when I read these words, I hear the voice of the priest-creator:

*I remark in passing that I believe it highly likely that there is some truth in the story of both the star and the Magi. Like the other infancy stories, if one is to believe the best scholars on the subject, it emerged in its present form from the liturgical dramas, arguably children's dramas of the early Christians. So the Epiphany plays in the primary grades of every Catholic school on the planet are even older than the written Gospels. The important themes of the story, which are what really matter, are that Jesus came for all and that we all must follow our stars. I suspect that the medieval pilgrims would have agreed if it were put to them that way. However, when one explains stories, one erodes much of their impact, a point that theologians often miss.*

So tonight I seek no explanations, just stories—and a Star.

*Non nova sed nove*: not new things but seen in a new way. Suddenly the familiar formula of St. Paul took on new meaning: "For now we see through a glass darkly, but then face to face." For years—alas, no longer—I had a framed reproduction of a favorite Rubens drawing, his early figure study of a young studio model for his first Antwerp triptych, "The Raising of the Cross." Seeing at the Met today the original now for the first time (all these years it had been no farther away than Harvard's Fogg Museum) confirmed my prejudice while underscoring how little prepared I had been for the glory of the original, with those dashes of white-chalk highlights over the torso that are never captured in a photograph. The last wall of the exhibition of Rubens drawings was titled "The Garden of Love." Ritchie had been lobbying me to include drawings from this show in my upcoming lecture with the same title. "Here they are," I announced, as two problems were simultaneously solved. At the end of the show was a room full of books, cards, and Rubens souvenirs. In the middle, I caught sight of my Rubens book. I was thrilled to see so many stacked copies—and then instantly prayed the pile would shrink over the next days! Authors never change their spots.

Tonight I sat once again in the Baroque sanctuary of St. Jean Baptiste, as the lay reader. The music, conducted by Maestro Somary, was Mozart's small jewel, the *Missa Brevis* in C, the so-called *Orgelsolomesse* (and appropriately the Maestro's wife played the organ solo, accompanying the voices of Amor Artis that filled the vaulted basilica). During these Mozartean moments, my eyes feasted on the huge, white, high altar, a wedding cake of neo-Baroque sculpture, until they rested on the monumental golden monstrance (empty during the Mass, but no less magnificent for the sacramental void). I had never before noticed that it included a gold statue of John the Baptist, patron saint of this church, standing in front of the stand, just below the gilded sunburst that radiates from the focal point where the consecrated host is displayed for adoration. He points upward toward the sacramental presence of Christ, as if to say, "Behold, the Lamb of God." Also unnoticed all these years was the golden garland of wheat and grapes—Bread and Wine—superimposed on the Bernini-like Gloria of light, golden shafts emanating from the sacramental Son.

When the time came for me to read the passage from St. Paul's Letter to the Romans, I found that I was hearing these familiar words for the first time—and for the first time, they made sense: the notion of being adopted children and heirs of God and coheirs with Christ; accepting our share of his sufferings so as to share in his final glory; and the entire universe of creation groaning in labor until its final release into rebirth. Somehow the music of Mozart and the latent glory of that empty monstrance brought to light the outline of faith as sketched by the Apostle. I sensed I had found, however dimly, as in the title of that wonderful Graham Greene story about an altar boy and a purloined host, "A Hint of an Explanation."

The city is hushed, covered in a deep blanket of snow—the first blizzard in several years. This morning, I emailed my son Chris three quotations from my mentor Jacques Barzun's masterpiece *From Dawn to Decadence*, his cultural history of the past five hundred years, published soon after his ninetieth birthday. When once asked how he was so prolific, he said he owed it to two main factors: insomnia and longevity. The quotations were to inspire Chris in comparing Savonarola and Luther. Only when I had finished emailing them did they strike me as particularly apt for our own time, in many ways as tumultuous as the era of the Reformation, when the world was rent asunder by religious zeal and fundamentalisms:

> A German scholar has recently argued that Luther never posted his theses. Whether he did or not, they circulated quickly; he had made copies and sent them to friends, who recopied and passed them on. Soon, Luther had the uneasy surprise of receiving them back from South Germany, printed.
>
> This little fact is telling. Luther's hope of reform might have foundered like many others of the previous two hundred years, had it not been for the invention of printing. Gutenberg's movable type, already in use for some forty years, was the physical instrument that tore the West asunder....
>
> The incipient revolution had defined the enemy: not the Catholic religion and its faithful, but the pontiff, his employees, and their hocus-pocus, that is, the trappings of worship. When the pope's bull condemning forty-one of the ninety-five theses arrived in Wittenberg, it gave Luther an opportunity for a demonstration: he burned it publicly, to the great delight, naturally, of the university students

*crowding around him. For good measure, he threw in some prescripts, the decretals of Clement VI, the Summa Angelica, and a few books by a colleague who championed the pope, Johann von Eck. "It is an old custom," said Luther, "to burn bad books"....*

*The Italian Humanists witnessed one fit of Evangelical zeal and it was enough. Toward the end of the fifteenth century, the monk Girolamo Savonarola roused the Florentines to a high pitch of devotion that led to the famous "bonfire of the vanities." Such a high ideal tension cannot be sustained by a whole community for very long, and when this one broke, the prophet was declared a heretic and burned at the stake with public approval. Savonarola had been too literal—too Evangelical—in using the words of Christ to convert the masses.*

I began to feel I was actually learning something about that religious reformer who destroyed himself through grandiosity, believing himself to be not only a prophet of the apocalypse but also the founder of a new Christian Empire with Florence as its capital. He reminded me of Robespierre more than of Luther. Woe to religious leaders who seek political power. At least this one redeemed himself on the gallows, as he sought to emulate Christ's passion.

This evening the gospel reading was the Beatitudes

according to St. Matthew. The homilist noted that Martin Luther had considered the Beatitudes an impossibility to keep. Albert Schweitzer considered them possible to keep for a limited period of time, perhaps at the end. Joachim Jeremias (a Scribner author) was quoted as saying they already presupposed grace: without God's grace, we would be incapable of any such virtue—or blessedness. The new translation uses the adjective "happy" instead of the older "blessed." I was reminded of Andrew Greeley's cycle of novels based on them: "Happy Are the Oppressed," "Happy Are the Peacemakers," "Happy Are the Poor in Spirit," and so forth. How blessed are we, I muse, to be able to keep alive a few archaic words. Imagine if the Beatitudes were known as the "Happys." It is almost as grim as the Wise Men or Magi becoming "astrologers" from the East. Not a happy thought, much less a blessed one.

At the noon Mass at St. Vincent's, I learned that today's Feast of the Presentation in the Temple was traditionally called Candlemas. Father Jones explained that in days of yore, it represented the end of the Christmas Season (a calendar still followed by the more traditional Anglicans). I finally understood the title of a phonograph album of medieval and Renaissance chants I had bought as a college student and still love replaying: "From Christmas to Candlemas." As I sat pondering the small gleam of silver above the Virgin's right hand, like a floral candle, that image of light or flame was given a new slant in the Old Testament reading from the prophet Malachi: "For who will endure the day of his coming? And who can stand when he appears? For he is like the refiner's fire, or like the fuller's lye. He will sit refining and purifying silver, and he will purify the sons of Levi, refining them like gold or like silver that they may offer due sacrifice to the Lord." Even in this new translation, as I hear in the mind's ear the accompanying melody and harmonies of Handel's *Messiah*, I am reminded again that words may evoke music, especially under soaring Gothic arches.

# ORDINARY TIME

As I lay resting this afternoon to the background broadcast of the Met Opera's matinee of *Pelléas et Mélisande* by Debussy, I read an illuminating article by Barbara Haeger on my favorite Rubens altarpiece, his "Epiphany"—or "Adoration of the Magi"—for St. Michael's Abbey in Antwerp. Her learned iconographical analysis cast this magnificent painting in new light as she cited the literary source of the glowing light that suffuses the composition to the Old Testament reading from Isaiah in the Missal for the Feast of the Epiphany: "Arise, be enlightened, O Jerusalem, for thy light is come, and the glory of the Lord is risen upon thee. For, behold, the darkness shall cover the earth, and a mist thy people: but the Lord shall arise upon thee, and his glory shall be seen upon thee. And the gentiles shall walk in thy light, and kings to the brightness of thy rising…." What words could be more uplifting after a dark, sleepless night?

I long for Lent; I am ready for it. This week, I decided I was more attuned to the evocative Gothic space of St. Vincent's than the bright Baroque of St. Jean Baptiste to the north, or the cozy cheeriness of St. John the Martyr to the east. Once there I realized, opening the missal, that this is the last Sunday of Ordinary Time, before Lent begins on Ash Wednesday, three days hence.

It was already dark outside by the time Mass began. But the gospel reading brought light: "You are the light of the world....Let your light shine before men so that they may see your good works and glorify your heavenly Father." Not a poor prelude for the upcoming season of fasting, penance, and good works. I pray I'll be ready by Wednesday.

On entering the church, a few dark images of the Old Testament flashed across my mind, footnotes to parental pain: the Flood, the Sacrifice of Abraham. But the reading today was the opening of Genesis, and the good pastor explained that we are given these two narratives of Creation in the two days before Lent as a reminder that when God created the physical world, he was pleased with it. "And he saw that it was good." So pleased that he took off a day, the Sabbath, for rest—not as a response to weariness, but as a period for reflection, contemplation, and pleasure. May that be my base line for Lent—a reminder that creation, for all its subsequent flaws, is essentially good: an original source of pleasure and something worthy of redemption. May that hope hold true for all parents—and for their children.

At St. Vincent's, the priest was late and I got an extra dividend: the silent enjoyment of the familiar church in a new light, the hushed tones and shadows of early nightfall, before the bright lights are switched on for the Mass. Gothic churches need to be visited more often in such shadows and the muted glow of polished wood, gilt, silver, and brass. After yesterday's homily, I heard the refrains of God's approval more clearly after each of the final stages of Creation. In this first account of the Creation story, the author simply says that God created Man "in his own image; in the divine image he made him; male and female he created them." It struck me that this primal vision clarifies the inclusiveness of God's reflection: both male and female partake equally of "his own image." The forbidding patriarchal image of the Creator was a later creation—of Man's. As I write, WQXR has just finished playing a recording of Elisabeth Schwarzkopf singing "Vienna, City of my Dreams": "*Wien, Wien, nur du allein, sollst stets die Stadt meiner Träumer sein....*" It's the very song I found myself singing softly as I walked from St. Vincent's to home. Why? I don't know. Music and beauty have their own promptings, unknown to us beneficiaries. But after hearing the recording that once caused me to memorize those lyrics, the announcer translated them and then added that the song was so beautiful it had to be repeated. I don't recall ever hearing an instant playback on this classical station, but it suits the night when Mardi Gras will pass silently into Ash Wednesday. I am ready at last for the fast.

# LENT

The evening Mass I reached on time, and in time once again for the clash of the gospel injunction not to "put on sackcloth and ashes" when we fast, but to "wash our faces." My ashes had faded since noon and an afternoon at the gym. But I resisted the temptation to get them imposed again; surely the gospel meant to discourage such conspicuous scrupulosity. The fast today was easy until I went to the store to buy Valentine cards; the profusion of candy and sweets finally made this day of abstinence and fast a real one. Lent always brings me back to my college years, when I first experienced it as a Catholic. It keeps me young—or, at least, immature.

When I got home, an email from the rector of St. Paul's School added a happy Protestant footnote to the day: "I am most impressed with Chris's piece on Savonarola as a precursor for the Reformation in Germany. Very insightful and scholarly." I have spent the last hour of Ash Wednesday writing to a fellow Rubens scholar about the finer points of Catholic doctrine regarding the "unbloody" sacrifice of the Mass as distinct from the bloody sacrifice on Calvary. So many religious disputes flow from the limitations of language. Our words may never capture God's Word. All our doctrines and Sacred Scriptures seek to convey the latter with the former—a heroic task that makes the notion of Lenten resolutions child's play by comparison.

Father Keitz announced that Mass today was in honor not of St. Valentine but of the brother bishops Sts. Cyril and Methodius, the ninth-century evangelizers of the Slavic lands. No wonder the Church is losing communicants if it cannot keep so simple a saint's day as Valentine's! Whoever arranges the calendar of feasts in the Vatican may be Roman, but no romantic—and even less practical. I recalled St. Teresa's fist-shaking exclamation to the Almighty as her cart was mired in mud en route to her newly founded convents: "No wonder you have so few friends if this is how you treat them!"

As I walked home, Robert Frost echoed silently through the trees—from his poem "Nothing Gold Can Stay." He tells us that Nature's "first green is gold"—the gold of the budding flowers that seem to last but hours, before they descend into leaves, as Eden fell into grief, and dawn dissolves into day: "nothing gold can stay." The very transience of Christo's "Gates," those industrial constructions of steel and blazing fabric through Central Park find a counterpart in nature herself, as in our experience of life after Eden. In two weeks, the Gates will be gone. Their intrusion is no more permanent than a temporary amusement park on a village green, or the acres of bright orange and black banners and tents that shroud the Gothic campus of Princeton each year for the week of reunions in June. I feel strangely cheered by this festive impermanence. Fireworks must be fleeting. When I reached St. Vincent's, I found the opposite, no less refreshing, above the statue of the Virgin: a dimmer light that gave a soft glow to her heavenward face while, at last, allowing the flickering candles below to outshine it. Nothing gold can stay. But it may be renewed.

Today I just had time to make the noon Mass at St. John the Martyr down the street before going to the airport to fly to Florida. The contrast of this 1950s neo-Gothic interior, no larger than most city chapels, and the vast cathedral-like interior of Goodhue's St. Vincent's could not have been sharper—yet I felt refreshed. Perhaps because I am enough removed now from the decade of my birth and earliest memories that I relish anything from the 1950s—a church as much as a film. The Mass is the ultimate rerun. The reading today was from the Book of Jonah. It took me back to the 1970s of the Aquinas Institute in Princeton where I heard this reading at one of the first early morning Masses I attended at the beginning of sophomore year as a newly minted Roman. I have often marveled at how vividly a book can transport me back to the time and place I first read it. I had not thought to include the less familiar books of the Bible in that musing—until today. Now I am off—not to Nineveh, but to Palm Beach; not in the belly of a whale, but in the bulkhead of a jet.

I got to St. Christopher's in Hobe Sound in time for a front pew. The reading from Ezekiel told of how God wants not destruction or punishment or death of a sinner but repentance. Father Kevin in turn told a charming story from his pre-seminary days, of how he once accompanied his bishop in a car ride to Miami and began to suggest to the prelate his candidates for excommunication. The wise bishop explained gently that he was not interested in kicking people out of the Church but rather in drawing them in. That is the Catholic model, the "here comes everybody" Church of Flannery O'Connor we need to uphold if we hope to survive this age of rampant secularism matched only by fanatical fundamentalism. The Old Testament's jealous God of vengeance is not Ezekiel's God of forgiveness and repentance.

As I entered St. Christopher's this morning, I noticed a new statue outside the side door: a guardian angel leading two children. No Bernini here, it's straight from Hallmark. Yet the spirit that motivated the banality was no less touching. Inside, two new golden sanctuary lamps, large and pointed, looked as though they may have been artifacts from a Cecil B. DeMille epic; the candle flames flicked so predictably through the deep red glass that I finally realized they were electric. Then, looking up between the stained glass windows of the nave, I caught sight of some ersatz tapestries hanging from brass poles: The Virgin and Child, Sts. Peter and Paul—all adapted from what once must have been classic images, again through the lens of a Hallmark translator. At this point of my visual meandering, I heard the gospel account of the transfiguration, a story and a vision that always take me back to my childhood church of St. Bart's and that magnificent apse mosaic reflecting the best of neo-Byzantine art, its forebears still gleaming in the apses of Ravenna and Mt. Sinai. But what struck me for the first time in hearing this familiar gospel story, a visionary miracle, was that ultimately it was not about sight, but sound: the voice of God proclaims the transfigured Jesus as his Son and tells us to "listen to Him." The priest, in his best Irish brogue, reinforced the message by reminding us how difficult, but essential, true listening is. As infants, we have no trouble crying; but listening is a discipline to be mastered—over a lifetime.

Back in New York, taking my mother to the evening Mass at St. John the Martyr, with far more sunlight along the route than a couple of weeks ago, has redeemed the day. It is the last day of Christo's saffron gates in Central Park; at the same time, it offers a reminder that the golden hues of "Nature's first green," according to the poet Frost, will soon be here in time for Easter. I have slipped so many times on my Lenten resolutions; I must remember those early days with my mother at the rink: the cure is to pick oneself up quickly, brush off the ice, and find the lost edge on which to glide once more. In my mind's eye, I saw again that recent photo of the pope standing at his hospital window to give his unique blessing to us all. Equally telling were my mother's words of gratitude for our little church of St. John Martyr around the corner. After hearing the gospel story of Jesus encountering the Samaritan woman—the ultimate outsider—at the well of Jacob, I no longer think of my mother as having to remain an Episcopalian outsider, a visitor—if now a regular one—to a Church where she now feels so at home. The Lord gives himself to all who approach with sincerity, just as he gave that puzzled Samaritan woman the water that would quench her thirst forever.

Today I sat again at Mass next to another lovely lady, Joan, this time at St. Vincent Ferrer: Joan Cuomo. I have not seen her for almost two weeks. The church glowed as the first snowflakes fell outside to melt on the sidewalks and streets. By evening, they would stick, as a hopeful image of Lent—and of faith. My Lent so far has not been a success: I have not stuck to my resolutions—too many exceptions, too much sloth. By afternoon, my back again feeling stronger after a cautious regimen of exercise, I returned to that church for confession. It turned into a splendid conversation with Fr. Keitz about the day's reading from the Book of Kings—my favorite Old Testament miracle since childhood:

the unlikely healing of the Syrian pagan Naman by the prophet Elisha. Its simple beauty lies in the illustration of God reaching over boundaries—our man-made limits—to extend his healing Spirit to anyone who asks: a prefiguration of Christ and the gospel of inclusiveness, a generous God in lieu of a jealous god. My penance is to perform some act of charity; a penance that sets the imagination free. The first image that came to mind was of Van Dyck's painting of St. Martin dividing his cloak with his sword in order to give half to a beggar. If I had a cloak, a horse, and a sword, I might be tempted to imitate him: *that* would surely stop traffic on Lexington Avenue! But whatever opportunity arises, it must be a private, quiet deed—perhaps, if I am lucky, one that may grow into a habit.

The Old Testament reading today was of Moses proclaiming a series of laws on the brink of entering the promised land. The gospel, in turn, quoted Jesus proclaiming that he had come not to abolish any of the Law, but to fulfill it. Father Keitz noted that Catholics and mainstream Protestants have been virtually silent on this latest case of church and state before the Supreme Court. Why? Perhaps because for us, those two tablets smashed by Charlton Heston in the epic film *The Ten Commandments* have never encompassed the whole of God's law. Indeed, our Lord himself condensed and summed them up in his two great commandments: "Thou shalt love the Lord thy God with all thy heart, mind, and strength, and thou shalt love thy neighbor as thyself." How strange, isn't it, that the born-again evangelicals, the fundamentalists who are striving so hard to place Moses' tablets in court houses, are not seeking to inscribe their inspired summation by Christ? These are not Christian inventions: our Lord quoted them from the Hebrew Scriptures. They are more inclusive—also more literally Christian—than the Ten Commandments. Nor is anyone fighting to inscribe the Golden Rule, surely acceptable to all humane religious traditions: Do unto others as you would have them do unto you. As a footnote to my meditation on these readings and his homily, I wanted to suggest still another biblical saying of Jesus to be placed in every courtroom: "Judge not, lest ye be judged."

Today on this "first Friday" of the month, Fr. Keitz asked the question, "How are we to love God?" He noted that the Muslims' chief prayer is "God is Great." Its simplicity has great appeal, although to me it will always have the haunting echo of the last words recorded by the hijackers just before they crashed into the Twin Towers. He then pointed to the first two petitions of the Lord's Prayer: "Hallowed be thy name"—that is to say, may we praise and glorify God; and "Thy will be done on earth as in heaven"— may *we* do God's will here. JFK echoed this call in his inaugural address when he said that "here on earth God's work must truly be our own."

Today I gave some new and needed thought to the source and meaning of the phrase "Light is the shadow of God," from which I took my last book's title. My father, the classics major, had introduced me to it in Latin, *Lux Umbra Dei*, as an inscription to post—for inspiration—on my senior thesis study carrel in the art library back in 1972. But I don't recall him ever telling me where he got it. Decades later, thanks to the Internet, I was led to Sir Thomas Browne for the English version. Just today I found that its source is, no surprise, in Plato, though I have yet to read it in Greek or discover the context. But long before Plato, the anonymous author of the Book of Genesis had reflected on the special relationship between light and God the Creator. The very first command of God's is "Let there be Light," the first act of Creation. "And He saw that it was good." In the New Testament, Jesus calls himself the "Light of the world." The Nicene Creed is even more explicit about the divine identity: Jesus is "God from God, Light from Light." But this Light is not a creation, not the light we know around us and described in Genesis. It is what St. Paul calls "unapproachable Light." Too bright for our imagination, much less our eyes. The English Renaissance philosopher Sir Thomas Browne framed this mystery as a paradox worthy of the metaphysical poets:

> *Light that makes things seen, makes some things invisible, were it not for darknesse and the shadow*

*of the earth, the noblest part of the Creation had remained unseen, and the Stars in heaven as invisible as on the fourth day, when they were created above the Horizon, with the Sun, or there was not an eye to behold them. The greatest mystery of Religion is expressed by adumbration, and in the noblest part of Jewish Types, we finde the Cherubims shadowing the Mercy-seat: Life it self is but the shadow of death, and souls departed but the shadows of the living: All things fall under this name. The Sunne it self is but the dark simulacrum, and light but the shadow of God.*

(from *The Garden of Cyrus*, chap. 3)

I am reminded of the similar paradox expressed by my favorite poet of that period, John Donne. In his sonnet "Death Be Not Proud," he concludes, "One short sleep past, we wake eternally and Death shall be no more: Death, thou shalt die!" But through my day's journey into literary sources, I stumbled upon a Victorian author, critic, and poet I had never before read: John Addington Symonds (1840–93). He composed a beautiful sonnet titled "*Lux Est Umbra Dei*" that sums it all up with sublimity:

*Nay, Death, thou art a shadow! Even as light*
*Is but the shadow of invisible God,*
*And of that shade the shadow is thin Night,*
*Veiling the earth whereon our feet have trod;*
*So art Thou but the shadow of this life,*

*Itself the pale and unsubstantial shade*
*Of living God, fulfilled by love and strife*
*Throughout the universe Himself hath made:*
*And as frail Night, following the flight of earth,*
*Obscures the world we breathe in, for a while,*
*So Thou, the reflex of our mortal birth,*
*Veilest the life wherein we weep and smile:*
*But when both earth and life are whirl'd away,*
*What shade can shroud us from God's deathless day?*

No wonder my father had given me that motto as I began to write my thesis about Rubens and the *Triumph of the Eucharist*. For that artist, as for Bernini and the other giants of the Baroque age, light was infused with metaphysical meaning. The sacrament in its golden monstrance blazes as a beacon of light, just as the Gloria explodes into golden shafts and gilded angels emanating from a stained glass window in Bernini's masterpiece in the apse of St. Peter's, Rome. No wonder Caravaggio included no painted apparition of Christ in his painting of the "Conversion of Paul" for Santa Maria del Popolo: for this revolutionary naturalist, light alone was sufficient to explain the divine source of Paul's blinding conversion on the road to Damascus.

I am used to God's coincidences as personal promptings. Even so, I was startled today when the lector, at the beginning of Mass, announced that this Sunday's theme of the Mass was "God's divine light." In Paul's Epistle to the Ephesians, we are told to become "children of light, for light produces everything good." In the gospel, Jesus grants sight to a man blind from birth. The priest in his homily observed that light was not only to be identified with sight, but with love. This notion of light as a medium of divine love, as a moral force, brings to mind the lovely poem written by Cardinal Newman during a sea voyage when his life seemed threatened by storms:

### The Pillar of the Cloud

*Lead, Kindly Light, amid the encircling gloom*
  *Lead Thou me on!*
*The night is dark, and I am far from home—*
  *Lead Thou me on!*
*Keep Thou my feet; I do not ask to see*
*The distant scene—one step enough for me.*

*I was not ever thus, nor pray'd that Thou*
  *Shouldst lead me on.*
*I loved to choose and see my path, but now*
  *Lead Thou me on!*
*I loved the garish day, and, spite of fears,*
*Pride ruled my will: remember not past years.*

*So long Thy power hath blest me, sure it still*
  *Will lead me on,*
*O'er moor and fen, o'er crag and torrent, till*
  *The night is gone;*

*And with the morn those angel faces smile*
*Which I have loved long since, and lost awhile.*

(At Sea. June 16, 1833)

No wonder these verses cried out for music; today we sing them.

Today at the Vigil Mass, a visiting Passionist priest, who is to lead the parish in a Mission, spoke of the Resurrection as a present event as much as a future hope—the resurrections we all experience in life, in all their facets, as gifts of God. This is our God "of second chances," as Father Greeley puts it so simply. I find myself praying Reinhold Niebuhr's famous prayer more often these days; with it has come an unprecedented degree of serenity. I need not be awarded a second Over-Anxious Parent Award. One such trophy is enough, and it sits proudly on my shelf, right beside that framed "Serenity Prayer."

The gospel reading about Christ raising Lazarus prompted a long sermon about death. The preacher, an Englishman transplanted to Florida, contrasted the views of the painter Munch and the philosopher Bertrand Russell (both of whom thought of death as no more than dissolution and decay) with the French wit—a monk manqué—Rabelais, who viewed it as a passage to *"le grand peut-être."*

He translated it today as "the great Perhaps." (A dubious destination.) But I couldn't help giving Rabelais more credit—the benefit of the doubt. The French phrase really means "the great Possibility" (or, literally, *Can-Be*). The English *maybe* is closer in spirit than *perhaps*. And that is true, for "with God all things are possible," as Our Lord reminds us. Can-Be has the force of potential, especially for a God who, in Tillich's formulation, is the "Ground of All Being," or "Ultimate Reality."

The priest then speculated about the possible cause of Jesus' being "greatly moved" at the sight of all the mourners around Lazarus's tomb. He explained that the Greek is more accurately translated "greatly upset" or even "outraged." He sided with the biblical scholars who interpreted Jesus' outrage as prompted by the effect of original sin, which brought death to humanity. But to me it does not ring true; that is the interpretation of a moralizing exegete. I wonder whether Jesus might more simply have been upset, even outraged, by the evident pain that Lazarus's death was causing his family and friends. Is it sacrilege to wonder whether some of it may even have been directed at himself? Jesus, we are told, had lingered two days after hearing that Lazarus had taken ill before making the journey to the home of Mary and Martha, Lazarus's sisters. Even if he could—and did—in the end raise Lazarus back to life and end the grieving, he must have realized that those four days of mourning—of tears and suffering—could have been cut in half had he come at once. Perhaps this speculation puts too human a face on Jesus; yet we read that "he wept." I think it was out of human (divinely human) compassion for his fellow mourners, not out of theological regret for universal sin.

I have finished the script for an introductory recording about my soon-to-be-published *The Shadow of God*. What a relief. Here it is:

> *I care nothing for birthdays; I consider my zip code far more central to my identity, and once claimed that my life's ambition was to die within it. But on turning fifty, I recalled my father saying, on his own fiftieth, "I feel as though my life is almost half over." As unforgiving time descended, the idea for this book was born. Not long before, at my parish church, St Vincent's—yes, in my zip code—I'd been arm-twisted by the pastor to give a Lenten talk titled "The Role of God in My Life." I never wrote it. The title was impossible. So I decided to wing it—on the wing of the Spirit, I prayed. What came out was the outline of a spiritual journey through a Protestant childhood on through my college conversion to Catholicism at the height of the Vietnam protests.*
>
> *I used as guideposts passages from books, plays, and poems that had fed my early spiritual life, and works of music that resonated into faith. I had heard and read—and taken for granted—that religious faith, or spiritual impulses, produced great works*

*of art—from the cathedrals of Europe to Handel's Messiah; but it struck me that the opposite is equally true: works of art nourish religious faith and spiritual growth. It's a two-way street. As Oscar Wilde quipped, art doesn't imitate nature, nature imitates art. Art—art of all kinds—shapes the way we view our surroundings, our world, ourselves, even God. As Bernard Shaw put it, "You use a glass mirror to see your face; you use works of art to see your soul."*

My dad liked to say, "No rush, just do it immediately." On the Feast of the Epiphany, the visit of the Three Magi to the manger, I finally decided to follow his fatherly formula for action. I started a spiritual journal, and journey, that would take me from Epiphany to Epiphany, over the course of a year, as well as back in time to my earliest memories. I've always had a special fascination for those Wise Men following their Star. In an early scene from one of my favorite novels, *Brideshead Revisited*, two friends, Sebastian and Charles, are having a dispute about Sebastian's Catholicism, which Charles dismisses as "an awful lot of nonsense."

> *"Is it nonsense?" Sebastian asks. "I wish it were. It sometimes sounds terribly sensible to me."*
> *"But my dear Sebastian, you can't seriously believe it all."*
> *"Can't I?"*
> *"I mean about Christmas and the star and the three kings and the ox and the ass."*
> *"Oh, yes, I believe that. It's a lovely idea."*

*"But you can't believe things because they're a
    lovely idea."*
*"But I do. That's how I believe."*

What has brought me back to this manger, time and
again? To Mass? To faith? What is the basis of personal
belief? How far back can we trace the roots of faith? How
deep are they? How were they fed? And—dare we ask—
who first planted the seedling? These questions pointed to
a journey backward into memory, to childhood, and from
there, as in one of my favorite films, "back to the future."

My earliest religious memory has me standing on a
New York street with my dad. I'm swinging my arms and
fists wildly. "What are you doing, Charlie?" he asks. "You
told me God is everywhere, right?" "Well, yes, but what does
that have to do with it?" "I'm hitting God." Not a promising
start on the road to faith.

Not long afterward, I met my first Catholic friend in
the first grade. He showed me the first crucifix I'd ever seen.
My response? "Let's throw it out the window and watch
Jesus fly!"

That year, my dad even took me to my first sunrise
Easter service, a true epiphany—not at the altar but off
to the side, where a network cameraman was perched
behind a huge TV camera. Why was he there at seven in
the morning? Something big was happening, for sure. My
father whispered to me that the entire service was being
televised. I had never seen a church service on TV, so this,
I thought, must be where CBS decided the action was that

day. And I knew right then that I wanted to keep coming back to church.

My favorite children's book, *The Tall Book of Christmas*, yielded treasure of its own, almost fifty years since I first opened its covers. I wonder whether that collection of stories with their colorful illustrations was perhaps the "first cause" of my choosing art history as my academic profession decades later. For me, art was never for its own sake, but a mirror—or window—on history, on worlds past, on Faith.

At college, senior year, my dad gave me an inscription to post on my desk: *Lux Umbra Dei*—"Light is the Shadow of God." Whether the light of the Star leading the Magi, or the blinding flash of light that converted St. Paul, or the light all around us each day.

In the same way, music, my first and lasting love, was never an abstract art. As a boy, I put a bust of Mozart in front of me on the piano, like Schroder's bust of Beethoven in *Peanuts*. The sounds were always rooted in the life of the composer. The printed notes seemed a diagram for a bridge between past and present as dazzling as the Golden Gate. To play or just to listen were two ways of crossing that bridge and entering another world. It remains a religious experience in the most literal sense of the word. The Latin root—*religare*—means "to tie together." Music forges the ties that bind us together, the living with the dead, mortals with the immortals.

And finally, the world in which I've spent most of my life by an accident of birth: books and authors. When I was fourteen, my dad paid me to read a list of books the summer before I went away to school—the best fifty dollars he ever spent. I can still recall where I was when I read each one—they have become part of my mental geography. The power of literature, of the mystery of written words "tied together"—religiously—is its ability to fuse itself with actual experience so that our memory, the mind's eye, makes no distinction. Books make it possible for life to imitate art—we see our world through a prism of words.

My son Charlie asked me, in the middle of this journey, why I had ever became a Catholic. I told him I was writing this book to find the answer. The French philosopher Montaigne once said, "I have no more made my book than my book has made me." This journey through memory, art, and faith shaped the year as it proceeded from season to season, from Epiphany, through Lent, Easter, Ordinary Time, Advent, Christmas, and back to Epiphany. It took me back to music, books, art, and worship as it quite literally tied together past, present, and future. It wasn't a year in Provence, or in Tuscany. I stayed close to my zip code most of the time. But by the end, I felt I'd been traveling with the Magi.

Yesterday, at the evening Mass of St. Patrick's Day at St. Christopher's, Father Hines, in his best brogue, gave an account of the emerald saint, comparing Patrick's charisma to Christ's: how otherwise could this medieval bishop have converted a whole island from paganism in one brief lifetime of ministry? As a prelude to communion, the priest softly sang in Gaelic an ancient Irish hymn, in lieu of the regular prayers, to St. Patrick. St. Augustine wrote that he who sings prays twice—a good note on which to end.

# HOLY WEEK

Back in New York, I took my mother to a more intimate church, St. John the Martyr. There we were handed palms, blessed by Monsignor O'Connor, before the long reading of the passion narrative, this year according to St. Matthew. How I wished for the shorter edited version; afterward, I was grateful to have heard it in full. Someday I must learn to reconcile patience with the passion.

This evening I indulged myself with Charlie's Christmas gift; I have been saving it for Holy Week—Bach's *St. Matthew's Passion*. I put the CD in the player, too late at night to listen to more than the first few arias and chorales, but enough to hear a voice that took me back thirty-three years. The soprano soloist, Ann Monoyios, sat next to me in music class at Princeton in 1972, the year she graduated. How could Charlie have known that the CD he picked out for me featured a fellow Princetonian? Nor would he have recognized the portrait of Bach on its cover as also from Princeton—from Mr. Scheide's collection in Firestone Library. But then, as Einstein wrote, "Coincidences are God's way of remaining anonymous."

This morning I returned to Princeton to pick up Chris at the Princeton-Navy crew races. Again Bach's *St. Matthew* provided the sacred music along the route for this day the Spaniards call *Sábado de Gloria*, the Saturday of Glory—far more evocative than our "Holy Saturday." After the long trip back home—was everybody driving into the city today?—I stopped off for a few quick prayers at St. John the Martyr. The church was dark, the tabernacle empty, but the Easter flowers and banners were ready for the Vigil Mass tonight. It all illustrated so perfectly the meaning of *Sábado de Gloria*, the darkness that heralds the light. Ritchie wanted to go to an Episcopal Church this evening, so we proceeded to St. James for the Easter Vigil. We gathered outside with candles and bells, followed the paschal candle into the church, listened in semidarkness to the *Exultat* and Bible readings interspersed with chants—it was far more medieval and Catholic than we Catholics can ourselves boast today. But I longed for some nice Protestant hymns, and then finally the lights came on in Easter splendor to the strains of the familiar "Jesus Christ Is Risen Today, Alleluia!" Home again.

# EASTERTIDE

Today I transplanted myself from the garden of the tomb, where Mary Magdalene mistook our Lord for the gardener, to the Garden of Love, up at the Met library, where at last I have the slides ready for my lecture. What a relief. Spring is in the air. The one remaining piece is to make a tape recording of the Countess's absolution of the Count at the end of Mozart's *Le nozze di Figaro*. I have chosen an LP from my early childhood of George London singing the Count with the impeccable Elisabeth Schwarzkopf as his Countess. After several tries, I finally got the heavenly absolution on tape. I missed Mass today, but Mozart provided the substitute. No wonder the theologian Karl Barth claimed that every afternoon, the angels sneak away from heaven's court composer, Bach, to play Mozart.

On my way, rushing late, to noon Mass at St. Vincent's, a beaming young lad stopped me on the street. I stopped, said hi, and then had to confess I did not recognize him. It turned out he was the younger son of one of my oldest friends, and I had seen him almost daily for years going to school with his mother. But in the past year, he had matured and grown into a sixteen-year-old that stumped the eyes of an art historian. I was dumbfounded that I failed to know him. On entering the church a few minutes later, I heard Father Keitz read the Gospel account by St. Luke of the Road to Emmaus, how two of Jesus' disciples on the day of Resurrection walked and talked with him along a long road without recognizing him—until he revealed himself "in the breaking of the bread." Their failure of recognition has long been a mystery, even to scripture scholars. But no longer to me. I now know how past images and expectations can blind the eye even to a familiar friend. They did not expect to see the glorified new man of the risen Christ; and so they did not. Only through the sacrament of the Eucharist were their eyes opened, as ours continue to be—if we consume it with open hearts.

I walked through Central Park to meet Father Owen Lee at the Paulist Church, just a couple of blocks from the Metropolitan Opera, where he will give his *Rosenkavalier* talk on Saturday for the matinee broadcast. As I crossed Columbus Circle, I caught a glimpse of the Mayflower Hotel now being demolished to make way for a new condo tower. So many Met opera stars stayed there between performances. It was there I heard the news that my first pope, Paul VI, had died. Now his successor is on his deathbed, according to the radio report this morning. Such morbid musings soon gave way to a three-hour lunch with Father Lee, at Fontana di Trevi, opposite Carnegie Hall. On the way, I asked the cab driver if he knew how to get to Carnegie Hall; he did: "Practice!"

I felt that I had known Father Lee for thirty years, not thirty minutes, by the time lunch began. Such is the power of his memoir, "A Book of Hours." He proved to be the shining exception to a warning given to me by my friend and editor, Michelle Rapkin. It was twenty years ago; we were young editorial colleagues at Macmillan: "If you ever admire an author exceedingly, be sure not to meet him." I am so grateful I have met Father Lee after so many years of hearing his radio broadcasts from the Met: he makes opera a sacrament.

Today, before venturing out, I indulged myself with the first act of *Rosenkavalier*. Father Lee's commentary of the "alomatic" aspects of this and other Strauss operas—how characters are changed by encounters with others, the opposite of an "automatic" change—struck an especially resonant bell today, as we await the tolling of those denoting the pope's passage into *eviternity*—that state the angels share as they have (unlike God) a created beginning, but no end of time. As I prepared to set off in my car to the gym, its battery went dead. So I put on my headphones and started to walk those few miles; a light drizzle soon turned into a steady downpour just as the news flash came that the pope had died. By the time I got to the gym, the televisions were showing live broadcasts from St. Peter's Square in the middle of their night. I couldn't help thinking of that line sung an hour or so earlier by the Marschallin that to stop time she would arise in the middle of the night and still all the clocks. But then she brushes off her vain whim with the profound insight that "we must not fear time…for it too is a creation of the Father who has made us all." The most beautiful philosophical refection ever elevated to eviternity by music: God bless Richard Strauss. The strangest, and most hauntingly beautiful, juxtaposition was looking up from my rowing machine to the scene on CNN of St. Peter's Square and the pope's lit window of his now-empty rooms while hearing Angela Denoke, a truly *angelic* Marschallin—the operatic rival to Jessica Lange as Angel in Bob Fosse's "All that Jazz"—sing those simple words of resignation and reconciliation on seeing her former lover Oktavian now joined, *für Evigkeit*, with his soulmate Sophie: "*In Gottes Namen.*"

A later report said that the pope's final word was uttered in response to the view from his window: "Amen." It is the purpose of art to reconcile us to life—rarely through preaching. In that conclusive blessing by the Holy Father, he reminds us that the purpose of our world, our surroundings, indeed life itself in all its beauty and banality, is to reconcile us to a higher realm than we can glimpse or even imagine. We must be grateful for those unexpected reflections in light, or echoes in sound.

Tonight Ritchie suggested we go to the seven thirty Mass at the Jesuit Church of St. Ignatius Loyola. A friend had told her the music was stirring, and she missed the music-filled Episcopalian services. I recalled St. Ignatius as one of the first churches I visited as a Princeton sophomore; I found it a dreary version of the Gesù in Rome. But over the past thirty-five years, thanks to a new organ and thousands of new wattage of floodlights, it now glows in midday splendor, even on a Sunday after dusk. The music was all she had been promised, a vibrant combination of organ, guitar, piano, percussion, and a Woodstock-worthy cantor, who also composed many of the Mass settings. The pastor was charismatic. But all of this paled against the realization, as I stared at the sanctuary, that here we were seated in the most Roman of all the New York churches at the very moment that the world's—at least the media's—focus was on the Eternal City, where the pope was lying in a casket waiting to be borne into St. Peter's tomorrow for the beginning of a week-long ceremony of mourning and a state funeral. The ciborium above the tabernacle here was modeled on Bernini's twisted, Solomonic columns of the high altar of St. Peter's, soaring above the grave of the first pope. I could not take my eyes off the mural behind the altar, illustrating in vivid colors St. Ignatius kneeling before the Renaissance Pope Paul III, who approved his new order of Jesuits. It was both a flashback and a preview of papal splendor to follow in the days ahead—all because my Episcopalian wife wanted to try something different. Another perfectly timed coincidence that made me smile at the twists and turns of faith along our pilgrimage.

This noon I was relieved to be back in the familiar Gothic surroundings of St. Vincent's. The Easter flowers, if a bit faded and wilting up close, still combined in radiant Easter splendor around the altar. Father Keitz explained that today we celebrate the Feast of the Annunciation, ordinarily set for March 25 (nine months to the day before Christmas), but that since that day fell on Good Friday, the Church delays it until the first "free day" following the octave of Easter. The flowers suddenly took on new meaning: those trumpeting Easter lilies are now also, today, the lilies of Gabriel's annunciation to Mary, so familiar from Renaissance paintings of that happy domestic scene when the conception of Christ is announced and accepted by Mary. I looked up at the silvery (tin) lily, one that will not fade, in the hand of the *Porta Coeli* (Gate of Heaven) statue of the Virgin. The postponement of today's Annunciation underscores those other annunciations of Holy Week, when this feast would otherwise have been celebrated.

On Holy Thursday, Jesus announces (in addition to the betrayal) the joyous institution of the Eucharist, which has brought us to Mass today as on any day for the past two millennia. On Good Friday, Jesus announces from the cross that the good thief will join him in paradise, but a still more stunning annunciation is delivered by an anonymous voice—that of the centurion at the foot of the cross after Jesus' death: "Truly this man was the Son of God." Then, on Easter morning, yet another annunciation: this time by an angel, completing the cycle of messengers, who announces to the women coming to the tomb to attend to the body of Jesus that "he is not here, he is risen." And then, just yesterday, the annunciation by the greatest doubter among Jesus' disciples, Thomas, who first proclaims the divinity of Christ, after his disbelief is shattered by the evidence in his own eyes: "My Lord and my God!" All of these annunciations during Holy Week and the Easter Octave are rooted in the one we celebrate today, the "prequel" that sets salvation on its course, a course that continues even with the death of our pope. After signing the memorial book in the narthex of the church, I took a card of John Paul II, with its papal blessing, and sent it tonight to my son Chris. Just before 9/11, we went to Rome together to see the pope, and we received his blessing at Castelgandolfo.

At the end of the noon Mass today, Father Carlton encouraged us to look at the memorial window to the pope at Bloomingdales—featuring a portrait of the deceased John Paul II. He never mentioned that it had been lent by our parish church. (It was, I have since learned, a gift to my friend and former pastor Boniface Ramsey.) When I got to the corner of Sixtieth and Lexington, I beheld the familiar vitrine now bare and painted a delicious pale yellow. On the wall hung a beautiful, gold-framed pastel of the pope; in front of it a simple but stunning arrangement of flowers. In gold letters on the wall was a brief salute to this "brave and beloved champion for peace," his dates of life, and an acknowledgment of the loan. I was never so proud to be a member of our Church, both universal and parochial. It was the most elegant memorial I have ever seen to anyone—all sunshine and light, like the smile on his face—and his spirit. Tonight, watching the three U.S. Presidents kneeling in prayer before the open casket of John Paul in St. Peter's, I felt the sadness of loss for the first time this week. Here were three men who have held the reins of worldly power, as head of the most powerful nation on earth, now joined in mourning their spiritual counterpart. Not one of them is Catholic; it makes no difference. Their faces said it all: this pope was everyone's pope; his death touches everyone as much as his life.

Today at the noon Mass, the new curate, Father John Thaddeus, told a story about amassing treasures on this earth— perhaps echoing the biblical saying that where your treasures are, there is also your heart. The story struck a chord.

A wealthy man and his son had enjoyed spending years on their art collection. Then the son went to war and his father shifted attention from the collection to concern for the fate of his only son. When the dreaded news came, it bore a silver lining: his son had been shot while rescuing another soldier, a heroic feat he had performed often—but once too often. A soldier arrived at the man's door carrying a package; after expressing his gratitude for the son who had saved his life, he told the father that he would like to give him something he had painted; it was a portrait of the son. The father, overcome, vowed to hang it over the mantle as his most cherished picture among the million-dollar masterpieces.

Not long afterward, the old man died, and his will stipulated that his entire collection, worth a fortune by now, would be auctioned off on a day associated with his son. A room full of excited bidders awaited the first offering: it was the soldier's portrait of his savior. His name meant nothing in the art world. Grumbling erupted into growls of complaints—"Can't we forget this junk and move on to the real pictures; this is just an amateur picture of the man's dead son, nobody wants it." The auctioneer quietly explained that by the rules of the auction that this portrait had to be the first sold. Didn't anybody wish to offer something for it? Finally, a man raised his hand and asked whether he would be allowed to bid ten dollars; he had very little money, but he knew the family over the years and admired the soldier son. Yes, replied the auctioneer, we have a bid for ten dollars. Do we have a higher offer? Some quiet snickering punctuated the embarrassing silence that was becoming stifling, until at last the auctioneer spoke those words of relief: "Going, going, gone—sold to the gentleman in the fifth row for ten dollars." Sighs of relief choked into gasps of confusion and consternation as the auctioneer added, "The auction is over." What do you mean it's over?

What about the millions of dollars of pictures in the back waiting for bids? The answer was simple: by the terms of the old man's will, the auctioneer explained, "Whoever takes the son gets it all."

The young Father John Thaddeus added that that is a pretty sound summation of the Easter message. At the conclusion, I was close to tears. Was it a projection of worry over the futures, even survival, of my own sons as they break into adulthood? Or was it a recollection of the time, a few years ago, when Father Andrew O'Connor came over to our new apartment and asked out of the blue what one object I would take with me from our home in a fire or similar disaster, with no time to ponder. Without hesitating, I replied, "That's easy—Ray Kinstler's portrait of my dad." In such an auction, I, too, might have been the only bidder; but even without the windfall, I would have won my prize.

As I headed southward toward the Bloomingdale's window, I saw it in a new light. An elderly nun was waiting for the new flower arrangements before taking a photo. A young woman and I started to stage-direct the prop men through the glass, to be sure they removed the florist's tag from the arrangements. That simple pastel sketch suddenly seemed more valuable—and more cherished—than anything in the neighboring windows featuring designer dresses with stratospheric prices. Love alters reason, calculation, appraisal, and judgment; it may even turn the world upside down. What a universal man he is, remarked the woman next to me, that this memorial window speaks to all the store's customers: not only to Catholics, but to Jews,

Protestants, Muslims, Hindus, Buddhists, to all religions and those of no religion. He's something special, she concluded. I could only nod.

Before leaving for Long Island, I paid my final respects to the memorial window at Bloomingdale's. The pope's funeral is over, but the networks replay the tape over and over. I finally see it—in a gym of all places. How strange to be exercising on a step climber while watching this stately service on the steps of St. Peter's. The vast arms of Bernini's Colonnade are filled with mourners great and small. The casket is of simple unfinished wood—a stark reminder of the essential humility of this saintly "servant of the servants of God," according to the pope's most telling title. Cardinal Ratzinger looks very papal as he presides over the liturgy: a prefiguration? We shall know within the week.

The church of John the Martyr could not have been a starker contrast to the fan-vaulted, stained glass reliquary of yesterday's royal chapel at Windsor—on television—for the marriage blessing of Prince Charles and Camilla. The Easter flowers were wilting, but the church was packed by the time my mother and I arrived, and spirits were high. The gospel today was my favorite, the Supper at Emmaus. As son Charlie hastened to complete his senior thesis in a couple of days at Princeton, the reading took me back to my junior year, when I wrote my spring paper on this subject in Renaissance art. For the past thirty-three years, I have heard that gospel story read each year, and yet always with a new slant of light cast upon the risen Lord.

Today it was not the miracle of the eucharistic recognition that caught my attention, though it is, as the priest explained, the heart of the story and indeed the miracle we all may experience each time we come to Mass. No, it was something I had never considered all these years. The two disciples were given the chance to have their eyes opened, to recognize the risen Christ "in the breaking of the bread" for one simple reason: they had invited a stranger to stay with them for the night and to share their meal. According to St. Luke, Jesus made it clear that he intended to keep going after the pair decided to stop for the night at that small village outside Jerusalem. He had spent a long time conversing with them, explaining the Scriptures to his downcast companions, but he did not ask for hospitality. He was prepared to keep on going into the night—where? We are never told. They invited him to stay and join them. They took the initiative, not he. Perhaps that is the very point St. Luke makes so clearly if subtly: if we want to see Jesus, we must ask him in; we must be prepared to invite the stranger in our midst. "In as much as you have done it for the least of my brethren, you have done it for me," he said earlier in his ministry. And he proved the point on the day following his resurrection. It is a notion as daunting as hopeful.

Back at St. Vincent's today, I was too distracted by the Gothic windows and the still bright but wilting flowers to pay attention to that heartbreaking sermon by the first martyr, St. Stephen, just before he was stoned to death. We are told that he had the face of an angel. Why would anyone stone such a young man? How could they live with themselves afterward? Perhaps that is the reason that Saul, who held the coats of the stoners, so soon became Paul, after he was struck blind and heard the voice on the road to Damascus. I wonder, did he see the shining face of Stephen in his mind's eye as he heard the accusing question of Our Lord, "Saul, Saul, why do you persecute me?"

I went to the Met this morning and ran into an art professor who was about to give a lecture on Rubens's houses, so I got a ticket and stayed. I have not seen Antwerp since 1977, the *Rubensjaar*—the artist's four hundredth birthday celebration—so it was an armchair travel treat, marred only by a passing remark that Rubens "was Catholic, but a nonbeliever." It was all I could do not to run up to the podium and call time-out. But I stayed in my seat and enjoyed the rest of the tour. (The only other off-note was in calling Rubens the "Donald Trump" of his city and time.) Afterward, I went up to the podium and said I hoped that I was the only one in the audience to have heard that remark about Rubens being a nonbeliever, as nothing was further from the truth. In the entire history of art there is arguably no more devout or believing Catholic Christian than Rubens—except perhaps Bernini in old age. Both went to daily Mass and practiced their faith in life as in art. The professor seemed surprised. Is it not possible, she asked, that Rubens might have wanted to appear a good Catholic in order to further his career as a painter for the Church? (How very New York and *au courant* to be so cynical!) Yes, I agreed, it would be possible in theory that an artist might pursue such hypocrisy for commercial gain, but there would surely be some evidence of it in his private life—his personal writings, his daily habits. In Rubens's case, an artist who was both a workaholic and a consummate businessman, it is inconceivable that he would waste an hour each day to attend Mass *privately*—unless he truly believed.

Yesterday, as I paid a final visit to the slide library at the Met to pack up my trays of slides for next week's lecture, I ran into a distraught lecturer who needed a Rubens allegory to pair with Vermeer's "Allegory of the Catholic Faith." I was still reeling from the idea that Rubens could be thought a "nonbeliever." Perhaps that prompted me to look for one of his Eucharist tapestries. I could not find the slide in the museum's collection, but then rushed to my personal tray of old slides and—*ecco*: "The Triumph of Faith" came up after a couple of random draws from the deck. It was, she said, exactly the image and subject she needed. Faith won the day after all.

Today CNN showed preparations being made for the election of the next pope by the College of Cardinals in the Sistine Chapel. The announcer mentioned Michelangelo's ceiling and its beauty. What he did not add was that this will be the first papal election in five hundred years with that ceiling as bright and fresh and colorful—thanks to its cleaning in the 1980s—as when Michelangelo put down his brush for the final time. I pray those fresh frescoes may inspire an equally fresh and bold choice for the next successor to Peter.

Tonight at Mass we prayed for the cardinals who begin their deliberation tomorrow morning. As my mother and I left St. John the Martyr Church, I mentioned to Father Baker at the door that by next Sunday, we shall probably have a new pope. "Well," he replied, "they haven't elected me yet—I'm still here." *Touché.*

This morning the cardinals locked themselves in the Sistine Chapel. I cannot stop thinking about Vienna and how wonderful it would be to have a Viennese pope. Besides, Cardinal Schönborn is the only one of the *papabile* I have met—and with more charisma, charm, and intelligence than any archbishop I've ever known. They say that at age sixty he is "too young." How strange. Perhaps a mandatory retirement age for the pope would permit a return to relative youth and vigor for the most important spiritual job in the world. Still, as I approach another birthday, the notion that sixty is "too young" is blessedly consoling.

Yesterday afternoon, our time, black smoke poured out of the Sistine chimney: the first vote produced no pope. At the Metropolitan Opera Guild luncheon at the Waldorf-Astoria, I watched a moving video tribute to the great Spanish soprano Montserrat Caballé; both her singing and her life are immensely poignant; the tributes from her opera colleagues, magnificent. But it was not until she herself spoke her words of thanks "from the heart" that I understood why. She spoke of feeling on stage as though she were "in church"—in another realm, another dimension. She has transported others because she herself was transported. Inside the hotel ballroom, we all missed hearing the church bells outside ringing the news of a new pope. When I learned that the choice had fallen to Cardinal Ratzinger, I had mixed feelings. I love the idea of the first German pope in almost a thousand years, but his staunch conservatism is worrisome. Will conservatism without charisma render the papacy irrelevant to our new century? He has chosen the name Benedict. The last Benedict tried in vain to end World War I. I pray our new Benedict will have more success in achieving peace in our time. If not, his selection may signal the end of European leadership of the Church. As a confessed Eurocentric, I find that prospect tragic. The embrace of Catholicism is indeed universal, but its cultural roots are

European; the Church is the successor to the Classical tradition. I hope that Benedict XVI will surprise us all, as John XXIII did, and breathe new life into an ancient office.

On the front page of this morning's *New York Times*, the image of our new pope looks papal indeed—an encouraging image that reminds me how often the office molds the man, as much if not more than the man shapes his office. Who would have expected Nixon the cold warrior to initiate détente with the Soviets, or Reagan to make peace with the "Evil Empire"? History has a way of surprising us. Two things today raised my spirits and my view of our new Holy Father. The first was the mention in his *Times* biography that his hometown in Bavaria was once in the political orbit of Salzburg, Mozart's birthplace and, even more striking, that each day he took off fifteen minutes to sit at the piano and play Mozart or Beethoven—a most encouraging attribute in a pope! The second was a remark by Father Owen Lee, whom I had called to discuss his brilliant radio broadcast about *Der Rosenkavalier* just two hours before John Paul II died on April 2. He said that he was surprised that no one in the press had picked up the possible reference in Ratzinger's chosen name as pope to the "*Benedictus qui venit in nomine Domini.*" Blessed indeed is he who comes in the name of the Lord. He added that when Brahms composed his first piano concerto, he inscribed that very quotation above the opening theme of the second, *adagio*, movement: *Benedictus....*

Today, the Feast of St. Anselm, Father Keitz gave us a brief sketch of this brilliant church father's life; I shall always associate him, or rather my first knowledge of him, with that spring religion course, freshman year at Princeton, when we read and discussed St. Anselm's famous ontological argument: that God must exist by the very definition of God as "that than which nothing greater can be conceived." Even the atheist Bertrand Russell conceded that the proof worked. But today I heard an even better quotation to pin on this saint: "Theology is faith seeking understanding." Where do I stand on this spectrum? I wondered, looking up at the stained glass in noonday splendor. A Doubting Thomist? That poor pun sums up my conflict between an attraction to the shimmering structure of reason erected to point the way to God, like the Gothic vaults of St. Vincent Ferrer, and the nagging doubt that any human constructions, however soaring or stunning, can stake a permanent claim to absolute truth.

Later this evening, before driving up to St. Paul's, I returned to the stage of the Met Museum lecture hall to give, for the first time in a dozen years, "The Garden of Love." The intimacy of the paintings was matched by an audience made up—mostly—of friends and family who mean so much to me. Many of them had heard the lecture before; tonight's was better thanks to a new finale—in sound not image: a passage from the 1950 recording of Figaro highlights, with Von Karajan conducting, and with George London in the role of the count begging forgiveness of the incomparable Elisabeth Schwarzkopf as the Countess, who in turn sings the slowest and most legato absolution ever pronounced through music. It primed me for the easiest five-hour drive I have ever had to St. Paul's, even though I did not arrive until after midnight. Along the way, I played Mozart's *Abduction from the Seraglio* and part of his *Magic Flute*, enough to make me wish the trip had taken longer.

Back in New York, I arrived late to the noon Mass, and found that I had missed reciting the very psalm that yields the words of the St. Paul's School anthem (what are the probabilities, I ask myself?): "I was glad when they said unto me, we will go into the house of the Lord...." I was, and am. But my faith was soon tested by the young priest's homily as, echoing St. Paul, he said we must distinguish between the essentials of our Catholic faith and the (changeable) incidentals, such as belief in limbo and private revelations. Unfortunately, he cited among the essentials—along with the divinity of Christ and the Resurrection—the Church's prohibitions against contraception, homosexual and premarital relations, and women priests. There, in a nutshell, lies the problem. To the vast majority of American Catholics, these issues lie not at the heart of our faith but at the center of the hierarchy's preoccupations. Our Lord spoke not a word about these subjects in any of the Gospels. What might he say today about our priorities?

This morning at a trustee meeting of a Catholic foundation, as I listened to the report of the Fra Angelico exhibition we are sponsoring at the Metropolitan Museum in October, I realized that it was exactly twenty years ago that I sat at the same table as we planned our first project, a symposium on the cleaning of Michelangelo's Sistine Ceiling—also at the Met Museum. Two decades later, we are making slow progress—backward—through the Renaissance! I wonder whether Merlin felt as I do. It's a most pleasant pilgrimage—"back to the future."

Today is the Feast of St. Athanasius. Father Keitz explains the role this father and doctor of the Church played in combating the heresy of Arianism. Arius had denied Christ's preexisting divinity, coeternal with the Father from before the beginning of time. I had forgotten that the Emperor Constantine, who liberated Christianity in the Roman world, was, like so many others among the Roman authorities, an Arian. As I pictured the Rubens oil sketch of Athanasius defeating Arius, standing over the prostrate body of the heretic like a victorious gladiator, I could not help but wonder whether our Lord himself might have qualified as an Arian, too: there is, after all, much in the Gospels to suggest that Jesus the man was not conscious of his preexistence in the Triune Godhead before his birth in Bethlehem. Perhaps these controversies of the early Church owed more to battles of Greek philosophy than to revelation and faith. In his earthly ministry as recorded by the evangelists, Jesus seems to have spent precious little time defining himself in such airtight theological terms. Perhaps that explains the current success of evangelicals today—and the public's benign neglect of professional theologians.

This morning I drove down to Princeton to attend the celebration of the Princeton University Press centennial with my son Charlie. The Press had been donated by my great-grandfather; Charlie and I are the fourth and fifth of our names to pass through its magnificent gate designed by Ernest Flagg, the donor's brother-in-law and celebrated Beaux-Arts architect.

Elisabeth Schwarzkopf, via CD, accompanied me on the drive, singing gloriously Bach's "Jauchzet Gott," then Mozart, and finally Beethoven as I crossed Lake Carnegie and pulled into the U-Press parking lot. I had a good half hour before the noon Mass in the chapel, and so I decided to pay a visit to my Bernini crucifix in the Art Museum. Perhaps it was the backpack I wore (I was planning to go to the gym after Mass) that prompted two "Old Guard" alums, for whom I held the museum door, to ask me whether I was a graduate student. Yes, I replied, as amused as delighted: "Thirty years ago!" Time stands still in Princeton. It turned out that they were both museum docents, and so we walked upstairs to the Baroque gallery, where I pointed out Malcolm

Forbes's Rubens of "Jupiter and Cupid" and explained that it had hung in his office facing his desk before he finally gave it up to Princeton. I then told of how I had acquired my Bernini crucifix in London thirty years ago and, four years later, transferred it from my Manhattan bedroom to Princeton as an indirect engagement present to my fiancée. They had both known my mentor Jack Martin, in whose honor I had made the donation (but not before it had been put to its original use, one last time, in a Good Friday liturgy in the University Chapel). One of the grads explained that he had been a Catholic priest before getting married and raising a family. The other turned out, by some divine coincidence, to be the very doctor who had treated my friend Freda Humphrey, who was also a museum docent and my landlady during grad school. Small town: I had kept that crucifix in her house on Cleveland Lane for the good part of a year.

At this moment, the museum's director, Susan Taylor, appeared and pointed out the recent acquisition hanging next to my crucifix: a magnificent oil modello by Bacciccia for his vast ceiling fresco in the vault of the Gesù in Rome. Bernini had worshipped in that Jesuit church each day and had played a key role in designing this roof-raising illusion in which the vault dissolves into an overflowing apparition of angels emanating from the blazing sun of Jesus' name "IHS"—the Jesuit insignium—an adaptation of Bernini's Gloria in the apse of St. Peter's. Yet I could not linger longer; it was time for Mass.

That museum detour must have primed me, for I spent most of the Mass gazing at and deciphering the rows of stained glass windows above the transept altar. I had feasted on these rich blue panes for over thirty-five years, but today—for the first time—they came into focus: I had never realized that they represented a visual narrative of the passion, death, and resurrection of our Lord. Reading upward, from left to right, they begin with the Last Supper and conclude with the Ascension, tomorrow's feast. It was all so simple, clear, and obvious. Why had I missed the point all those decades? Because I had assumed that the scene on the lower right, beside the crucifixion, was the annunciation. It certainly looked like it. But today I realized that the young Mary before the angel was not receiving word of the Savior's conception but the news on Easter morning that the tomb was empty—an annunciation, to be sure, but not the first. As my dad liked to quip, the obvious is much overlooked these days. Indeed I had overlooked it for thirty-five years—and three degrees in art history.

This afternoon Ritchie and I went to visit a recently widowed friend and watch the Kentucky Derby with her. As I sat looking at the big screen and took in the thousands of expectant onlookers, I felt decidedly detached. I had no stake in the outcome; all the horses and riders looked like winners before the race, and I had no favorite. Whatever the outcome, I would cheer the winner. Does God have favorites? Is every day Derby day for the human race? Or is he as divinely detached? Einstein quipped that "God does not play at dice." But what about horses? Is it enough to say, along with St. Paul, "I have run the good race"? Perhaps the running is more important than the winning.

This morning I left my zip code early: jury duty. The last time I served was Holy Week 2001; I had read the New Testament while the clock ticked in the assembly room. I finally opted out of a drug trial on Holy Thursday. What will happen this time? I think it is time to serve justice. During the lunch break, I went to St. Andrew's for Mass; the solid Georgian brick church stands between the federal court-house and the municipal building. Even at one o'clock, it drew a significant congregation. But then trials have a way of sending people to God: how many of my pewmates were defendants? (Or their attorneys?) I spotted one court offi-cer in the congregation. All stand before the altar as equals. The interior, with its dark mahogany columns and pan-eling, presents an ecclesiastical variation on a courtroom. Where the judge's bench might stand is the altar; in lieu of the inscription "In God We Trust" looms a life-sized bronze crucifix of the dead Christ. "He trusted in God," as one of his mockers noted. Such trust is no insurance against suf-fering or dreadful judgment here on earth; it looks beyond pain and the grave. It outlasts death itself. That is the only trust worthy of God, and of his Son who bore our collective punishments "once and for all" on that cross.

This morning the final jurors were chosen; I am the first alternate. My penance may be the obligation to listen to the entire trial but to remain mute, unless a juror falls by the wayside and I move onto the panel. The case is fascinating: a murder with a defendant who sits in the dock on the basis of witness identification. It raises that difficult question of recognition: the problem of Emmaus and Mary in the Garden on Easter morning. Except that here a man's freedom or conviction of a capital offense hangs in the balance. The defendant has very sad eyes: Are they windows to the soul, or a mask?

The victim was a heroin dealer; it is easy, too easy, to be dispassionate about him, and about the crime. He was dealing and was shot in the head outside a schoolyard, just before the children were dismissed. The young man who witnessed the shooting—and claimed to identify the killer—was my son's age; but already he had four children (the first at age seventeen) and several drug arrests. Police witnesses provided clinical testimony; the murder seemed surreal, artificial, staged for a TV drama until a seemingly unimportant witness took the stand—a Hispanic woman who was picking up children at the school when the shooting broke out. She thought they were firecrackers. When she emerged from the school and saw the staggering victim calling for help, she rushed over to him; he collapsed on top of her; she called for 911, then cradled his bleeding head in her lap until the medics arrived. Her description conjured up a Caravaggio *Pietà* as it might have been painted in the lower east side of our island across the Atlantic, four centuries later. She broke down sobbing on the stand as she relived her simple act of charity to a dying man—"one of the least of these my brethren," according to St. Matthew—and then explained how she followed the body to Bellevue hospital and met the family while he lingered on life support. Afterward, she went to the stranger's funeral. She had answered the question posed to our Lord, "Who is my neighbor?" That question, back then, elicited the parable of the Good Samaritan. Today it is illustrated with poignant and chilling pain in the face of the saintly home-healthcare worker who leaps into a role cast for Mother Theresa. She knew nothing about the victim's background or street business; he was simply a wounded soul in dire need of compassion; she gave it in abundance. All the while I kept thinking in the words of Oscar Wilde that life imitates art, not the other way around. This was a real Pietà—an evocative configuration of sorrow and compassion. I could only envy the children and old people she had assisted professionally in their homes and through the most mundane tasks. It's rare to see a saint on a witness stand; but today I believe I have. I only wish I could thank her for her humanizing gift to us all this day in an otherwise seemingly heartless court of justice.

# PENTECOST

Today is the Feast of Pentecost; as I grow older, it grows in significance. The Holy Spirit has always seemed, to me at least, to run a distant third in the Trinity recognition race—except among Pentecostals. She deserves better. Today the priest at St. John the Martyr wished us a "happy birthday" at the beginning of Mass. It is, he pointed out, the day that marks the birth of the Church with the gift of the Holy Spirit in a rushing wind and tongues of fire. The flowers around the altar are stunningly ablaze in hues of red and orange. It is a glorious way to herald the coming of summer and new beginnings. That is the most precious of all gifts of our faith: the promise of endless new beginnings, whether through the sacrament of absolution, redemption, or just the gentle breath of the Spirit, the whisper of second chances renewed.

Today was the last day of testimony in the murder trial. The most surprising and potentially devastating of the prosecution witnesses was saved for last: a woman of thirty-eight years, the mother of twelve children, who claimed to identify and remember in a fleeting view of no more than a few seconds the defendant wiping blood from his face as he strode past her a few blocks from the murder on that day in June two years ago. She was firm in her identification, but I remain troubled, knowing that I could never remember any stranger's face with such certainty. I have so often recognized faces in a crowd that turned out to be wrong; I do so every week or so, despite a trained eye that can distinguish a Rubens from a copy. I would not convict a man on such illusory powers of recognition. I would insist, like Thomas, on putting my finger into the nail prints. I want physical evidence, not an apparition. Whether I shall have a chance to share my convictions of doubt remains, alas, dubious: all twelve jurors showed up in the box today. I still sit outside, the first alternate. I hope I am not the defendant's only hope.

The final day of the trial—all twelve jurors took their seats, leaving us alternates outside the box to listen, but only listen, to the concluding arguments. The defense attorney did a valiant job of highlighting all the inconsistencies of the prosecution witnesses, but at times, he protested too much. The inconsistencies of details, recollections, descriptions were no greater than those of the four Gospel writers; the inescapable conclusion was that they did indeed witness the same central event and captured its significance. The prosecutor, following up, did an even more brilliant job of fitting all the pieces of evidence together and showing how all the witnesses, even when subject to the lapses of observation and recollection, reinforced each other. In fact, those very inconsistencies were cited as evidence of the desire to be truthful; these witnesses no more tailored their testimony to conformity than did the earliest editors of the Gospels. I left the courtroom with a new sense of peace, no longer minding that I would not be given a chance to deliberate. My distrust of eyewitness identification or recognition remains intact, but in this case, it no longer reaches the level of reasonable doubt. I believe the prosecution has proven its case; so I can finally accept any verdict by my twelve colleagues. During our lunch break, before the judge's final instructions, I sat in Javits Plaza with a juror, a visiting nurse, and as we chatted, I spotted a tall, young man with blond hair crossing the square in front of us. He stood out of the crowd. I mentioned that he was someone I saw in the gym every week although I didn't know his name. Fifteen minutes later he returned in the other direction, or so I thought. But suddenly I was no longer sure. Was this jacketless young man in the bright blue shirt the same one I had pointed out earlier? She said yes (I had not noticed the color of the shirt). Well, then, I replied, I must have been wrong: I don't think it is the person I thought it was after all. Not from this new angle. Then it struck me: this is the very problem at the heart of the case that she, but not I, will have to decide.

I dreamed last night that the jury was still out, after days of deliberation. I shall hold off calling the court until tomorrow to give them more time. Meanwhile, we must explain to son Chris our reasons for ruling out his taking a trip to China and Tibet this summer. Not every country subscribes to the presumption of innocence—especially for American teenagers! We also must explain that our verdict is final; the murder trial seems so much easier in hindsight.

I called the court this morning and learned that the jury had returned with a verdict of guilty several days earlier. So much for dreams.

This evening I took my mother to St. John's after returning from Long Island. The Pentecost banners were still ablaze, along with the birds of paradise and red lilies from last week. Today is Trinity Sunday. Father Baker defined the Trinity as a "mystery"—pure and simple—as inexplicable to us mortals as the mechanics of computers and cell phones are to the nonscientists, that is to say, most of us who use them daily without really knowing how they work their magic of communication. But something else struck me as I looked up at the crucifix, the altar, and the banners of the Holy Spirit in tongues of fire: I usually find myself praying to God the Father, the first-named member of the Trinity, the One who most easily personifies the abstract notion of God. Yet the Father is the one person of the Trinity with whom we have no immediate contact. The

Holy Spirit dwells amongst us, with the Church; Christ, the Son, is still as present in the sacrament of his body and blood, the Eucharist, as he was in human form with his disciples two thousand years ago. There are no visions of the Father; in the Creation myth of the Garden, he is said to have walked this earth—but not since then. No, he is the remotest of the Trinity, despite—for me at least—being foremost in the mind's eye. Why does he choose to reveal himself—to "present" himself—only through the Son and the promptings of the Spirit? That seems an even greater mystery than the notion of the Trinity itself on this Trinity Sunday. Perhaps that may be the very reason for the Trinity as the formulation of our most mysterious God.

# ORDINARY TIME

Arising at the crack of dawn in Princeton, we drove over to the university and got to the head of the line for commencement exercises two and a half hours before it began. It was like lining up for a papal audience at Castelgandolfo with my son Chris several years ago. The payoff was when they let us in, and Ritchie, Elizabeth (Charlie's girlfriend), and I got front row seats facing Nassau Hall. I had plenty of time to reflect on my own three graduations there. It felt odd, for once, not wearing an academic gown. But being in the audience for the first time in a generation offered a new perspective—*non novum sed nove*: not something new, but seen in a new way.

The diplomas are framed; the photos developed. Seeing these documents under glass, with snapshots in hand, reminds me how much I rely on visual cues to trigger elusive memories, especially happy ones. As an art history student, I first heard that "the eyes are the windows to the soul." It was a reference to portraiture, that we glimpse through the sitter's eyes (at the hands of a great painter like Rembrandt) his, or her, soul. But now it strikes me that the converse is equally true: it is through our own eyes—

whether looking at a work of art or even a snapshot—that we may reach into our soul and re-experience our deepest memories. This evening I arrived late at Mass to hear the priest reading a long passage from the Book of Tobit. It too brought me back to my student days, to the many representations by Rembrandt of the blind Tobit, who was cured of his cataracts by his son Tobias with the help of the angel Raphael. Sight and insight: how much the one owes to the other.

Last night at dinner—just four of us: Ritchie, my mother, Charlie, and I—Charlie announced that he hoped to be engaged to Elizabeth by the end of the summer, with the wedding a year from now. I was stunned; he has just graduated and has not yet begun his job in Birmingham. Then today at the five thirty Mass at St. Vincent's, I heard the conclusion of the Tobit story: how his son Tobias is brought together with Sarah in marriage. She had been widowed seven times on her wedding nights—hardly a promising record. Yet Tobias persists, saying that their marriage is ordained by God. Just the message I need to hear today: who am I to second-guess Providence?

Before going to bed last night, I mailed a card from my mother and me to a friend who has been diagnosed with pancreatic cancer that has already spread to his liver and thyroid. Rob is going into surgery on Tuesday, determined to save his life. Mom enclosed a check for the surgeon's fee, since he is worried his insurance will not approve it. I am incredulous that surgery will make any difference, but in the end I conclude that the gift is worth the price of hope—even an unreasonable one. Like the jar of ointment that Mary spent on Jesus to anoint him before the passion, it seems—as it did to Judas—an extravagance. But such acts of faith are never wasteful if they spring from true charity, that is, love. I looked for Joan Cuomo at Mass today, but she was away visiting her sister. The prior gave the homily on this Feast of the Sacred Heart of Jesus—one I have never really grasped, as it reminds me only of all those saccharine images so alien from my Episcopalian rearing. He transformed the image from a pseudo-valentine to substance as he recounted his own early doubts and anger as a new Christian with a God who seemed so remote from human suffering. Where is God in the midst of all such horrors? With his Son—on the cross—in our midst.

At Mass this evening, the priest talked about our present-day problem of grasping the notion of sin. He pointed out that the Hebrew word for sin, and the Old Testament notion thereof, meant literally "missing the mark." The idea is that we fall short, like an arrow, of the target of our potential, God's expectation and design for us.

I find that notion of sin more useful than the layers of Christian piety that have through the centuries attached themselves to the word, like so many barnacles. But perhaps I am looking for easy consolation for accumulated shortcomings. Still, it seems more practical to correct mistakes than to alter one's existential state. The genius of Catholicism has been its willingness to be practical and persistent in matters of sin and penance.

Late last night, just before dropping off to sleep and avoiding hours of waiting up for our son, I came upon the most arresting, challenging, and strangely consoling comment of our new Pope Benedict. When asked about the diplomatic maneuvers that eventually fell apart and resulted in the excommunication of Archbishop Lefebvre some twenty years ago, and specifically whether the then Cardinal considered it one of his failures in office, he replied, "I do not judge myself in terms of successes. My conscience is clear...I did what was possible." Such a simple, tranquil examination of history and conscience offers a true epiphany. We must not judge ourselves in terms of successes; and, in all fairness, I apply that rule to my children. (I am reminded that Patrick Hemingway, son of our family's most famous author, once told me, "Remember, children are not responsible for the way their parents turn out!") It is not the outcome, but how we approach it, that surely counts in the eyes of a loving God.

At St. John the Martyr, the Gospel was from St. Matthew, stern and yet oddly encouraging. I never can listen to this Gospel without picturing, from forty years ago, that stark and powerful Pasolini film—with Christ, in black and white, reinterpreted by a brilliant agnostic. At the beginning of the passage, we are told that to be worthy of Jesus we must prefer him to our own family, even our own father and mother. I think it would be easier to pass through the eye of a needle. Yet following this harsh prerequisite is the extravagantly generous promise that if we welcome a prophet, we earn a prophet's reward. All we have to do is to welcome him, as did the couple who set up a small rooftop room for the prophet Elisha. On the way out of church, I mentioned to Father Baker at the door that I never realized before that Elisha had been given a penthouse. Yes, he quipped, and equipped with a lamp!

At Mass today I felt tired and distracted and in no mood to listen to Abraham's incessant bargaining with God over how many righteous souls would be enough to spare the city of Sodom from destruction. Perhaps it tapped into a wellspring of bargaining with teenagers over the years. Yet it shows a more patient and tolerant side of the Old Testament God than we often envision. Abraham was a royal pain—for a good cause, granted—but Yahweh yielded in the end. May he continue to do so, and more often than I.

One of St. Matthew's harsher edicts, in the voice of our Lord, rang through the midday Mass: let the dead bury the dead. It seems too heartless, unless the command was rightly aimed at those who had a special gift for tackling the challenges of life and living. He did not want them distracted. When his turn came to face a corpse in its tomb, what did he do? He called it out by name, and Lazarus was reborn. That Gospel urges us to look forward, not back to the grave of mourned failures. Father Carlton quoted the famous story of St. Teresa d'Avila, whose cart got stuck in the mud en route to a convent she was reforming. Bespattered by mud, unable to make progress, she shook her fist heavenward and exclaimed, "No wonder you have so few friends if this is how you treat them!" (Out of the mouth of a saint and doctor of the Church.) So we may be pardoned for such dark thoughts in these days of natural disasters, illness, terrorism, and wars. Yet she persevered, and the message today is that I must not do any less. That is the price of discipleship. Onward.

Following a sleepless night, I stumbled into the noon Mass at St. Vincent's to hear the gospel account of the paralytic who after long years of suffering and immobility, comes to Jesus to be cured. Jesus forgives his sins. When challenged by religious leaders as to his capacity to forgive sins, he then tells the paralytic to take up his mat and walk. And so he does. The order, it would seem, is first faith, then forgiveness, finally healing. The paralyzed man must have had extraordinary faith in Jesus' reputed powers to come to him as a last resort, after so many years of illness. And, of course, he must have been willing to ask the help of others first; how else could he have approached Jesus in those days before wheelchairs? Some friends must have carried his litter, or portable bed. By the end of Mass, out in the street and in the bright sunlight of midday, it finally dawned on me that the only persons we have any power to reform are ourselves.

Today at the village church of St. Gertrude's in Bayville, I reflected on Pope Benedict's concerns that liturgical reforms have gone too far and have lost too much of the worship of God at the center of the Mass. Perhaps it may be true somewhere, but for all the Vatican II simplicity in this vernacular and prosaic liturgy—something I have grown accustomed to during the past thirty-five years as a Catholic—I find nothing here lacking in dignity or humility of worship. The music, to be sure, a combination of guitar and flutes, resonates with more spirit than tonality; but I can always hear other notes in the Scripture readings. The first, from Zechariah, "Rejoice greatly, O daughter of Zion; shout for joy, O daughter of Jerusalem; behold, your king comes to you," prompted a private echo of Handel's great soprano aria at the beginning of *Messiah*. Then the gospel account of Jesus telling his disciples that his "yoke is easy and his burden is light," took me back again to that same oratorio, this time to the chorus at the end of the Christmas section. Today it was not music herself, but rather the Word that begat music. And that is cause enough to rejoice, and not to lose heart in what was accomplished in the reforms of Vatican II. I can no longer imagine myself—much less this new generation of Catholics scattered about the church— sitting through a long Tridentine Mass each week in Latin, to the accompaniment of Gregorian chant. The liturgy must stay attuned to the times—and attention spans!—if it is to remain true to the Word: "My yoke is easy, my burden light."

The Old Testament reading at the noon Mass today cast an equally redeeming light on recent experience. ("Experience," said Wilde, "is the name we so often give to our mistakes.") It was the story of Joseph sold into Egyptian slavery by his jealous brothers, whom he much later encounters when, unrecognized by them, he has the opportunity—as Pharaoh's minister—to alleviate a famine back at home. They are dismayed when he suddenly reveals his identity to them, but he assures them that he forgives their selling him into slavery since it was, in the end, the means by which God used him to avert starvation among his people. He was chosen to save the chosen, however obscure the means might have so long appeared. I have never heard a better example of *ex malo bonum*, of good emerging from evil—until, of course, the Cross. This small epiphany led me back to a sacramental renewal of that doctrine. *Ex malo*: from sin we arrive at absolution, and the chance to begin anew.

This evening I watched with son Chris his new DVD on the life of Dietrich Bonhoeffer. I was both touched and inspired by his interest in that wartime martyr. I had had no idea that the theologian had been inspired by his experience here in New York of the Black Baptist Church in Harlem—what a stark contrast to the formal, intellectual tradition of German theology. But what struck me as much, and more disturbingly, was the dark seductive power of all those newsreels of the early years of the Nazi regime. Before their evil was fully revealed, they orchestrated a magnificent masquerade of order and restoration in a country ravaged by chaos and despair. What a terrible misjudgment the Vatican made in signing a concordat with the Devil to protect the freedom of the Church in Germany. But in charity, Pacelli—like so many Protestant counterparts—was duped into thinking that Nazi passions could be tempered by the influence of the Church. Our modern century would prove so much more malevolent than those so-called Dark Ages of fifteen hundred years ago. It took a Bonhoeffer to remind the world of what stuff a saint is made. What better role model for my Catholic teenager? How much we still need Bonhoeffer's sense of a common ecumenical cause. Perhaps our new German pope, whose faith was forged in the same furnace of totalitarian evil, will prove as timely—and timeless.

I was still thinking of Bonhoeffer and those images of the Third Reich rallies as I listened to the reading from the Book of Exodus at today's Mass. The description of Pharaoh's army being swallowed up by the waters of the miraculously parted Red Sea, as directed by DeMille, offers a disturbing image of divinely ordained mass destruction. Was there no other way of ensuring the safe passage of Moses and his chosen people? The New Testament reading of our obligation to choose Jesus even if it means rejecting our own families presents no less harsh an image as the price of salvation.

Today I passed by the latest quotation on the message board of Christ Church, Methodist, on Park Avenue. It is from St. Augustine: "If one is to value Christ at all, once must value him above all." No exemptions permitted: the sea must engulf all forces of opposition. It sounds so alien to that Greek motto, a favorite of my dad's, *méden agan*— "nothing in excess." God alone may offer the ultimate antidote: excessive forgiveness.

This morning son Chris and I drove down to Princeton to have lunch with the Provost, Chris Eisgruber. A distinguished scholar of constitutional law, he believes in a strong, activist judiciary as a guarantor of democratic freedoms, particularly religious freedom. He said he had been raised a Catholic—the religion of his Bavarian forebears—schooled in a rigid Catholicism that I, as a convert, had been spared. Yet we both found our ultimate academic field by fleeing an undergraduate course in anthropology. Ten years apart, we owe that department an accidental debt.

As we discussed the ideological debate over how the Constitution is to be applied, I kept thinking of the Bible—so central to our faiths, yet so potentially divisive in how it is read and revered. If it is to be the Living Word—not an artifact of religion—it must be probed anew for its underlying message of eternal truth. It cannot be taught as a textbook of cosmology, biology, or even religious rules (a redundancy). The two extremes—deconstructionists and literalists—are both deadly; the comparative degree hardly matters: poison is poison. Our separation of church and state has resulted in a vibrancy of professed and practiced faiths (plural) not to be found anywhere else in the world. Those firebrand evangelicals who would tear down that wall of separation do so more at the expense of religious freedom than of godless secularism. The fastest way to empty churches—as Europe has proven—is to make them state-sponsored shelters. God's house—the realm of angels and archangels, cherubim and seraphim—is not a department of motor vehicles, or passport office.

Last evening as my mother and I were about to get up from our pew at the end of Mass to leave St. John the Martyr, I noticed what looked like a small round badge or piece of cardboard on the seat between us. It was bland, no larger than a poker chip. Too insignificant to bother picking up. But Mom kept pointing to it and so I picked it up and only then realized that I was holding in my hand a host, the body of Christ. Someone must have brought it back to the pew. How often, I can't help thinking, do we leave the Lord unnoticed in our midst—right beside us? The new message at the Christ Church signboard yesterday proclaimed that religion is something one does, not something one waits for. My dad would have agreed; he always said that deeds matter more than feelings.

The Mass at St. Vincent's this evening included the story of the Israelites complaining to Moses that the "miraculous manna" that had rained down in the desert to prevent them from starving had lost its taste and appeal; they grumbled about all the good food they had to eat in Egypt, even under slavery. Moses, in turn, scolded God. He said he would rather be granted a quick death if this is how God intended to treat him and his chosen people. I find the honesty refreshing; prayer was in those days a candid dialogue, lacking pious hypocrisies and pandering worthy of Uriah Heep. When the priest returned to the altar after distributing communion, he took a sudden fall forward onto the marble floor of the sanctuary; everyone gasped, and many stood up ready to spring to help those servers who were helping him to his feet. The paten of unconsumed hosts had gone flying, the sacrament scattered over the marble floor. As I watched the reader, the server, and eucharistic minister—all laypeople—gather up the strewn hosts, I was reminded of those many Renaissance paintings of the "Gathering of Manna." The scene had suddenly been updated and moved indoors; the pieces of miraculous food were now the sacramental body of Christ, the promised source of eternal life. Once the priest had clearly recovered from his fall, the image of that latter-day gathering of manna took on a new light. We, too, so often grumble; yet we gather. There really is no choice. The food is too precious to ignore.

Late last night I got an emergency call from Chris. He was supposed to have arrived in Nantucket; instead he was calling from an airport motel in Georgia. He had boarded the wrong plane in Newark, unnoticed by airline personnel, and just when he thought he was landing in Massachusetts, a voice announced over the loudspeaker: "Welcome to Savannah!" This morning I awoke at five to give him a wake-up call, so that he would not miss his plane north. By midday he was in Nantucket. He gives new meaning to the idea of returning home "by another route."

At the noon Mass, celebrated in honor of the Blessed Jane of Aza, mother of St. Dominic, I finally learned why the Dominican Church is full of images of a dog carrying a torch in its mouth. When she was bearing her first son, Dominic, she had a dream that she would give birth to a dog carrying a torch, a reference to the fiery message to be carried around the world by the founder of the order of preachers, Dominic, whose name in Latin (Domini-canis) means "dog of the Lord." The English phrase "hound of heaven" sounds more poetic, just as his mother's name, Juana—in Spanish—seems more blessed than Jane: even Joan or Jean or Jeanne sounds more melodious. But let Jane have her day; I have had mine.

I sat next to a real Joan today—Joan Cuomo; my pew neighbor is back. Later today, another Joan, my mother, returned from a trip north in Cazenovia. So the Joans may claim this day—perhaps that settles the preferred translation of Dominic's blessed mother. This morning I received a copy of a clear forgery of a letter supposedly by my mentor, the late Julius Held, authenticating a so-called Rubens oil sketch in Madrid. The forgery was awkward, the art references equaled by the number of grammatical and spelling lapses. (One should forge only in one's native tongue.) I have left a message with the art dealer here in New York who has the letter; I do not want to tip my hand; I said only that I want to discuss the painting and Professor Held's opinions with him. I have long wanted another art crime adventure: perhaps this will be an opening. Meanwhile, two great pianists have just played on WQXR the first Schubert impromptu I learned almost forty years ago; how many more signals do I need to hear or see before I return to that other keyboard and start practicing again? I am notoriously lazy during summer months;

the rhythms of the academic year have not faded. Perhaps by September I shall finally get back to music in a serious way again. I know down deep that I ignore its promptings at my own peril: she is a Muse I dare not neglect for long, for she loosens the knots of the soul.

Today I got a letter from my late mentor Julius Held's daughter, Anna; it was a photocopy of the purported letter by her father "authenticating" a Rubens oil sketch in Madrid of the Last Judgment. She is certain it is a forgery, and she is right. Julius, like so many of his fellow scholars, came to America in the 1930s to escape Hitler and his thugs. English was his second language and he spoke and wrote it plus-perfectly. The Spanish forger needs a strong dose of Berlitz. I contacted the German representative of the seller here in New York; to his credit, he had sought to have the letter verified once he discovered that Held was deceased. He emailed me photos of the would-be Rubens: I was relieved to see that it was as bad as the forgery, an amateurish copy of a masterpiece in Munich. I told him to pass along the word to the owner that I was turning over the forged letter to the new head of art crimes at the FBI; that news should stop the culprit from taking Held's name in vain again.

At Mass I saw that today is the feast of the dedication of Santa Maria Maggiore in Rome. I have always felt a special tie to that ancient basilica dating back to the time of Constantine, for it is the first of the early Christian churches that I discovered in my first art history course at Princeton. Its nave is lined with fifth-century mosaics illustrating scenes from the Old Testament in vivid simplicity, a foreshadowing—by over fifteen hundred years—of Matisse. Now I want to hop over to Rome and see them again, and renew the visual connections to faith that I have neglected recently. I need to reconnect with art history in a direct way; I also want to return to the early Christian sources that so captivated me on my first trip to Rome—months before I was claimed by the Baroque. Perhaps I can lure Chris or Ritchie back there too—but even a solitary visit would be fine, for I would not be alone. That twenty-year-old who first saw Rome in 1971 is still with me; I'd like to see the Eternal City again through his eyes.

At St. Vincent's I learned that today was the Feast of St. Dominic, and the homily was all about his image as a "dog of God." The priest took the metaphor a bit further than I had expected, with lots of explanations about the training of a good bird dog (one that doesn't eat the bird before returning to its master!). But it struck me as timely, since our puppy Cha-Cha had just completed her annual series of shots by the vet, less than an hour before Mass. She now weighs slightly over five pounds, but she is a bundle of perfection. No wonder St. Dominic is hailed as a *domini canis*!

A package arrived from the composer and former choir director (when I was a student) at St. Paul's, Robert Powell. It contains the published score for the new anthem I commissioned for the school's sesquicentennial—in memory of my father. Set to the words of the school prayer by Powell, it is titled "The Joys of Life." I had suggested that title, lifted from the prayer, to highlight the enduring happiness that comes from service to others. "Grant, O Lord, that in all the joys of life we may never forget to be kind. Help us to be unselfish in friendship, thoughtful of those less happy than ourselves, and eager to bear the burdens of others, through Jesus Christ our Savior. Amen." I read this prayer at my father's funeral almost ten years ago (he had forbidden any eulogy). Today those words still resonate; I cannot wait to hear them sung to Maestro Powell's music.

Today I heard the harrowing Old Testament reading about the king who had promised to sacrifice the first person he saw on coming home to battle, only to be greeted by his only, and beloved, daughter. He had to keep his vow: Father Peretsky, the prior, explained that promises made to God must be kept, and that is the origin of the second commandment—do not take the Lord's name in vain. I thought first of Mozart's *Idomeneo* as I heard the story, then during the homily, Graham Greene's *The End of the Affair* and Robert Bolt's *A Man for All Seasons*. Oath taking, promises made to God, can cost a life. The remarks about sacrificing children—and the repulsiveness it evokes today, as then—struck home. In any parental struggle, the temptation to give up (or give in, more often) confronts the horror of sacrificing a future, perhaps a life, in so doing. This has been a tough week. But at the back of the church, the custodian Robert insisted I take a copy of a paper on his desk: it was a step-by-step guide to forgiveness! And it made the point that forgiveness is not a feeling, but an act of will. As my dad used to say, "Actions are more important than feelings." The priest who wrote this guide evidently agrees.

Tonight at the movies: the film *March of the Penguins* documents the instinctive pains that these adorable creatures endure each year to guaranty life for their offspring at the coldest point on the globe, the Antarctic. Their monogamous bonding and sharing of duties put us humans to shame. We should be so good. But the film also sheds new light on my "Over-Anxious Parent" award displayed on the shelf for the past five years: the penguins substitute action for anxiety—a good lesson to learn at the movies on a sultry Saturday night.

Late last night, before going to sleep, I read some more of an early prayer journal by Father Greeley; it dates back more than a dozen years ago. During summer days like these, he was at his vacation house in Grand Beach, outside Chicago, pondering the mysteries of evolution and God's role in creation. The film about the quasi-human rituals and instincts of penguins casts the question in new terms, especially during the current debate over the teaching of evolution vs. "intelligent design" in our schools—the subject of a *Times* headline this weekend. Who knows what role God intended evolution to play—or indeed what role penguins play? It's a grand mystery being played out each day before our eyes, a show that has had a long run indeed, and we pray a longer one—if we latecomers to the planet don't burn down the theatre! Greeley also probes the question of whether—as the Hebrew prophets believed—God suffers from, and for, and with, his human creatures "created in his own image." The Greeks, echoed by most Catholic theologians, thought otherwise: a perfect God does not grieve. We cannot cause him to suffer. Yet the crucifix behind the altar at St. Gertrude's this noon offers a stark rebuttal. Jesus wept and he suffered—for us. And if, as our Creed dictates, the Son is coeternal with the Father, from the time before time, then the capacity to feel pain, to suffer, to experience compassion, predates humanity, and surely remains part of the divine attributes today (unless we believe that the Risen Christ is less than his earthly self).

My father once told me that the cross has lost its shocking aspect; we would see it more clearly if it were recast as an electric chair or gallows, with the condemned suffering his final, gruesome fate before our eyes—and in church. That is what so clearly differentiates the Christian sanctuary from the Holy of Holies. In the Hebrew temple, God was curtained off and dwelt behind the veil of the tabernacle. Now he hangs high, in all his naked suffering, before his worshipers. If God could do so much for us in the flesh, who may claim he does not suffer still? Perhaps in that suffering through and for his creation, we may recognize our ultimate hope. Fear and awe have lost their edge in our postmodern world; pathos may be our last remaining path to salvation. Like those penguins confronted by new mountains of ice, we must find our way through.

I burned a lot of fuel today as I drove out to the end of this long island and back. I was never so grateful for a cell phone: a long-distance friend guided me through winding country roads on my way homeward, as I sought to bypass the bumper-to-bumper traffic along the main route. What if the Magi had had cell phones? This other route was a godsend. Once home, I saw the morning's paper: on the front page is a prominent article on scientists trying to evaluate the place of religion in our universe of theory and fact. The leading question is simple: "Can you be a good scientist and believe in God?" The answers cover the spectrum of belief and disbelief. Clearly the scientists who do believe in God bear the greater professional burden. But even more important is the question of the role of God within a cosmos of scientific laws. He can no longer be relegated to the role of "Fudge Factor." But if his laws hold true, even the laws of random theory, then must he be relegated to the Deist's image of the clockmaker who steps aside and lets the clock tick away according to its own mechanisms? If he enters our world, then how?

Separating science and morality as two distinct realms offers no satisfying answer. The relationship between Creator and creation, or Lover and Beloved, must remain a mystery—one that we are forced to confront and grapple with, like Jacob and the Angel. Perhaps this quest to solve the mystery at the heart of existence and of consciousness defines our humanity. We too may become Wise Men—if only we have the heart and stamina to stay the course to the manger and back.

The images in the news today of the devastation caused by yesterday's Hurricane Katrina are beyond a Bosch or Breughel of apocalyptic destruction: once again Nature has outstripped art. As I sat in the medieval sanctum of St. Vincent's, I felt a world away, as indeed I am. Yet the same God rules over both the destruction and the peace of this earthly Jerusalem: How can it be? That is indeed the great mystery—and tragedy—of life, the ultimate test of faith. Yet if Father Greeley is right, God dwells at the center of all human suffering as well as in the eye of the hurricane. The source of all life and love knows no bounds; perhaps because he has willingly bound himself to creation with all its flaws. Perfection rests in the future, a promise and a process, not a past or even present. *Ex malo bonum*: good may spring from evil, as resurrection from crucifixion, as birth from labor, and life from death.

This morning the continued reports of the aftermath of Katrina prompted me to call Elisabeth Schwarzkopf. I have been meaning to call for several days to confirm that I have my flight booked for December, in time for her ninetieth birthday. My father's dictum "no rush, just do it immediately" takes on new meaning in the wake of Katrina. We had a long and happy conversation and she said that she would find me a hotel nearby in Schruns, and that we would go together to the concert in honor of her birthday. She is still recovering from her fall, but I pointed out that she has a full three months ahead and that she is the most resilient person I know. She warned me that I must not be surprised to find that she is now "very old"; I thought of the thirty-year-old Marschallin at the mirror with those same thoughts, as I replied, "Your soul, like your voice, is still young—and will remain so." And she laughed, "Let us pray that will be so."

How strange that today of all days, September 11, the Sunday Mass readings all speak of forgiveness. First the prophet Sirach tells us that vengeance belongs to God alone; we mortals are expected to forgive each other if we ourselves wish to be forgiven by God. Then Jesus tells Peter that it is not enough to forgive seven times, but "seven times seventy," which in Hebrew parlance of the day meant an infinite number. That formula is given its most economic form in the Lord's own prayer: "Forgive us our sins as we forgive those who sin against us." Late this morning I had a long conversation with Aunt Patsy that took a detour into the subject of forgiveness (of course, in hindsight, I now realize that she had already been to church, and was considering the same lesson of the day). As I drove into New York and reflected on the subject further, I thought the ultimate prize to be earned in life would be this: to be judged "forgiving to excess." Only at the day's end, as I picked up the *New York Times Magazine* with Bin Laden on its cover, did the last piece fall into place. Can the vengeance of 9/11 ever be supplanted by forgiveness? That would be a miracle.

Today the theme is discipline, so hard to practice after weeks, even months, of neglect. I forced myself to make the phone calls and appointments—boring things like fixing air conditioners and washing windows—and then set aside an hour before the noon Mass to get back to practicing the piano. Knowing I had just that hour made it easier, a reversion to the habits of a schoolboy who has only one free period between classes. But just returning to pieces first studied more than forty years ago felt good. The idea is to get started and pray that momentum will take over.

My reward was one of the best weekday homilies I have heard—about a man whose profession was discipline: the Roman centurion who commands large numbers of men by the strength of his orders, but who reaches out to

Jesus to have his sick servant healed. When Jesus decides to come to the centurion's house in person (no doubt the Roman expected our Lord to achieve the healing miracle by the strength of his verbal command alone), the soldier comes out to dissuade Jesus from entering his house: he says he is not worthy for Jesus to come under his roof, "but only say the word and my servant shall be healed." Jesus is astonished by the Roman Gentile's faith, and the servant is found to be healed.

Father Carlton explained why this centurion is so attractive a character in Luke's Gospel: first, his care and concern for his servant; second, his utter faith in Jesus and understanding of our Lord's power; finally, his humility. These three together compose the essence of Christianity, of what we are called to practice: care for others, faith in the Lord, and humility. Those words spoken at each Mass before the reception of communion today find a lasting context as they glow with new light: "Lord, I am not worthy to receive you; but only say the word and I shall be healed." The lesson of the centurion makes me want to persevere; let's see how resolute this newfound discipline will be tomorrow.

This morning I crossed the Park toward the Met Opera, where I hoped clouds of concern might be dispersed by a working rehearsal of the Verdi opera I know least: *Falstaff*. It did not disappoint. This comic opera by the old Verdi—his last—about proposed adultery and cuckolding by the buffoon Sir John Falstaff (based on Shakespeare's late play *The Merry Wives of Windsor*) transfigured the theme of marital infidelity into true comedy, where relationships are resolved and restored to equilibrium, to a state of grace. The sets by Franco Zeffirelli are stunning; the singing and acting by Bryn Terfel in the title role, perfection. It was a rare working rehearsal—in full costume and full voices—that actually covered the whole opera, even with corrections and repeats by Maestro Levine (listening to him fine-tune the orchestra and singers is almost as good as Verdi's music). There was, for me, a most welcome footnote, literally: the first scene of the second act ends with a ringing brass flourish on the tonic chord that echoed my favorite Verdi fanfare (in my favorite Verdi "opera")—the triumphal last notes of the Sanctus in his *Requiem*, following "Hosanna in Excelsis!"

I was hoping that, in this case, those sacred notes preceded their recapitulation in Verdi's comic masterpiece, a work that I first heard decades ago but never appreciated until today. A quick Internet search confirmed the order of flourishes: Verdi had written the *Requiem* twenty years before his final opera. I am reminded that it took me several hearings, three decades ago, before I fully appreciated the *Requiem*, which then became my favorite piece of choral music. Now, as repayment for this epiphany today, I must listen more closely to the opera. I have just ordered a copy of the Gobbi-Schwarzkopf-von Karajan recording from the mid-1950s. I want to savor Schwarzkopf as a radiantly witty Alice Ford before I visit her in Schruns. Another Alice—a decade later and here at the Met, was just as beautiful in the role and as funny as Lucille Ball—Mary Costa. She told me it was one of her favorite roles, and that the opera itself is a "musician's opera." There is not a wasted note. I left the opera house with that sense of hope and redemption from the ultimate Author of comedy—a sacrament. "*Siete un gran seduttore!*" Mistress Quickly sings to Falstaff—"You are a great seducer." So is Verdi—so is God. This is one seduction to which we may all safely succumb.

This morning in Boston, the sight of the red-covered Gideon Bible in the top drawer of the hotel bedside table reminded me of a Bible quotation I have been meaning to look up for several days. I had done a favor for an old friend who then responded with a blessing from Isaiah, my favorite Old Testament poet-prophet. The verse cited was 58:11, and I was determined to remember it by whatever means available (I had no pen or paper at the time of the phone call of thanks). So I thought, I'll associate this blessing with Easter and Thanksgiving, which follows it as a calendar holiday: my first remembered Easter was in 1958 (a most memorable televised service at St. Bart's to which my Dad took his six-year-old son) and Thanksgiving—the appropriate response to the Easter miracle—is celebrated in November (month eleven). Corny, but it worked: days later I opened the Gideon, the first time in my life I have ever used this hotel edition as a reference book, and found the verse: "The LORD will guide you continually, and satisfy your soul in drought, and strengthen your bones; you shall be like a watered garden, and a spring of water, whose waters do not fail." No wonder I have always preferred Isaiah to the Psalmist.

We drove up to St. Paul's to take son Chris and his friends out to dinner. Chris questioned me first about a host of religious writers and philosophers whose work I no longer recall from school days: from Descartes to Kant. He is taking a course called "The Challenge of Unbelief"; he wants me to give my proof of God's existence (as in St. Anselm's ontological argument: "God is that than which no greater can be conceived.") or, failing that, my basis for belief. He argues that the burden of proof is on the believer. I don't see it that way, but I must confess that I have not given the problem as much thought as my seventeen-year-old.

I tell him that I don't believe we can prove God's existence any more than we can prove our own: yet I prefer to accept my existence and that of those around me than to admit that all our reality may be a dream. What, then, absent proof, is the basis for my belief in God? I suggest that the answer may lie in my book *The Shadow of God*. Chris tells me it does not (has he really read the unpublished manuscript on my computer?). He may be right; I must pursue it further—here. Perhaps this may prove another route by which to return home.

Chris asks whether I think that in a thousand years our descendants will be surprised that we still believed in a God behind the universe; I counter that if mankind is still around, our descendants may—after so many centuries of further scientific discoveries—marvel that we had such a limited view of God. In the meantime, I suggest to him that faith is like a scientific theory: it cannot claim to be absolute truth. But it can propose to explain the data in a more economical and elegant way than alternative theories—the idea of the "beauty" of a scientific theory that accounts for more with less. Our Christian faith, I propose, offers a model for existence—for the universe in all its complexity (pain and joy, evil and beauty) that gives life richer meaning. Yet I am not willing to settle for Sebastian Flyte's claim to believe in something just because it is "a lovely idea."

The choice of belief must be rooted in something deeper than aesthetic appeal. Perhaps it is like believing a witness during a trial. I believe in God because I choose to believe the testimony of Jesus, and the corroboration of the saints. If, as may be counterargued, Jesus was delusional or just mistaken, well, then I'd rather fall with him than separate myself from him. That is the ultimate question of belief—and challenge of faith: In whom do we place it?

Back in Boston, Ritchie and I walked almost three miles from the hotel to the Museum of Fine Arts. It has been five years since we were last there—and almost forty years since my first visit as a third former at St. Paul's, when our class was bussed there from the north to visit the Egyptian wing. That is where Ritchie wanted to start our tour, for she is researching Egyptian mummies and artifacts for her latest student tours at the Met in New York. But, as in 1965, I could not wait to escape down the hall to the European Old

Masters. Ritchie has little admiration for my unrepentant *Eurocentrism*. But that is who I am: a product and devotee of the Classical tradition rooted in Greece and Rome and baptized by Christianity.

I saw the one painting I came to revisit: Rubens's finished oil sketch, a *modello* for a tapestry of "The Sacrifices of the Old Covenant." I first saw this magnificent painting in the dining room of its owner at his Georgian country house in Topsfield, Massachusetts—thirty years ago. But today it looked three hundred years younger. It has been thoroughly cleaned, all the layers of yellowed varnish stripped away, and now it sparkles with whites and fresh colors right off the master's palette. *Non novum sed nove*: not something new, but seen in a new way—an epiphany enough for the twenty-fifth Sunday in Ordinary Time.

Upon arriving home I found at our doorstep a package containing the EMI 1956 recording of *Falstaff* I had ordered before heading north. I have not yet had time to play it, but I read John Osborne's enticing introduction. He quotes, in conclusion, the philosopher Susanne Langer—a name I recognized from the list of my father's authors—asserting that "comedy is an image of human vitality holding its own in the world amid the surprises of unplanned coincidences." By this definition he calls Verdi's *Falstaff* "comedy's musical apogee: the finest opera, inspired by the finest dramatist, by the finest opera composer the world has known." Dante called his great journey through hell, purgatory, and heaven the "Divine Comedy." It is how I want to see the world, all creation, all of life's vicissitudes, with its darkest shadows as well as scorching light: a work of art that will prove, in the end, to be comic not tragic. It is why I have always preferred the former to the latter as entertainment; at its most inspired, it may become a sacrament.

I look forward to my homework: listening to the masterpiece I missed as a student. In encouraging Verdi to take up his pen one last time—and for the first time in comedy—his librettist Boito wrote, "There's only one way to finish better than with *Otello*, and that's to finish triumphantly with *Falstaff*. Having sounded all the shrieks and groans of the human heart, to finish with a mighty burst of laughter—*that* will astonish the world." Verdi did, and it still does.

I have begun Thomas Woods's apologia for our Catholic heritage. He seeks to redress what he considers residual anti-Catholicism in popular culture and academe. Woods offers a readable, lively—if polemical—synthesis of cultural history. Beginning in the Dark Ages, we read of the monks who, according to Christopher Dawson, kept the light of learning from being extinguished. In dealing with barbarians a millennium and a half ago, Dawson notes, "The Church had to undertake the task of introducing the law of the Gospel and the ethics of the Sermon on the Mount among peoples who regarded homicide as the most honorable occupation and vengeance as synonymous with justice."

Woods's book reminds me of Kenneth Clark's series "Civilisation"—and of Lord Clark's eventual conversion to

Catholicism. Woods cites historian Will Durant, an agnostic, speculating that the barbarism and brutality of the Dark Ages, following the fall of Rome, might have been "worse had not the Church maintained some measure of order in a crumbling civilization." A dinner companion once asked the novelist and acerbic convert Evelyn Waugh how he could possibly call himself a Catholic and be such an insufferable human being. Waugh replied that it was only being a Catholic that kept him from being so much worse.

I decided to drop into my childhood church, St. Bart's. A small chamber chorus was rehearsing a Bach cantata. I sat down in the front pew. The music was entrancing. No wonder Karl Barth said that in heaven Bach is the court composer. No composer, not even the divine Mozart, has ever surpassed him in the realm of the spirit. He is the master of all. Once the musicians dispersed, I learned that I had been listening to his "Wedding Cantata"—about enlightenment and heavenly light. So it was. *Lux Umbra Dei*: music may best capture that light that is the shadow of God, especially in a darkened church on an impromptu visit.

Today a young Dominican friar gave a long homily on the feast of the angels—it used to be called the feast of St. Michael and the Angels, or Michaelmas. He began with the story of the angel sparing Rome from the plague and the surrounding army of the invading Lombards fifteen hundred years ago under Pope Gregory, which was later commemorated by the crowning statue of St. Michael brandishing his sword atop the Castel Sant' Angelo, that Vatican fortress and armory where so many subsequent popes took refuge. But then he launched into a sociology of angels and heavenly history based on apocryphal legends: how Lucifer rebelled when he was shown God's plan of salvation and refused to share a place of honor in heaven with the Virgin Mary. He concluded by asking us how often we prayed to the angels: not at all, I thought to myself. Perhaps I am too monotheistic at heart. I envision a new bumper sticker: "God is My Guardian Angel."

Last night I shared my journal entry with a friend and physician who likes to tease me about my adopted "upper-case Catholicism," which offsets his preference for "lower-case *catholicism*" (with a dose of anticlericalism not unusual among those born into the faith before Vatican II). I told him that I don't mind his enjoyment of *The Da Vinci Code* as long as he reads it as fiction and not as history, as alas so many are doing; also, that as a convert I was spared the rigorous Catholic indoctrination as a child that he has spent his adult years fleeing. Today I received his reply:

> *Your daily meditation made me think about angels…*
> *again! In truth I think about them a lot. Lest you*
> *think I have thought of donning robes let me explain.*
> *Indeed, it is true that the good priests—and the bad*

ones—instilled me with all that was Catholic and little that was catholic. Why not, for example, tell me that the greatest Seder ever known was the Last Supper? What else would a good Jew be doing on that day but celebrating Passover? Instead I was only given the version that makes it "we Catholics" and "all of them non-Catholics". Eventually, like the proverbial mustard seed, I found comfort in the hard surface of the wayside. Ironically, I flourished on the dry soil because it was less filled with the manure of doctrine. So, that takes me into angel...not by word association but by apologia.

Some years ago two events collided or conspired to bring me to angels. I was working with a man who was gay and having problems coming to terms. Being a Muslim, he felt that he would be doomed as per the Koran. We spoke at length about the Koran, and I was surprised to learn that the Muslim faith has angels. Since there are angels in the Kabala as well, it got me to wondering about this common thread. So there I was faced with angels facing East, some around me like good Catholic guardians, and others perhaps donning the beards of the learned Rebbe. (By the way, I relieved his anxiety by telling him that "it was written" that he be gay and therefore acceptable to his God.) Back to angels: one of my patients called and insisted that I read Dr. Weiss' book Many Lives, Many Masters. To my amazement it dealt with angels, although the author may use a different *term. If you have not read it, I would add that to our Theological Cocoa…if yes, I welcome your opinion. Frankly, it gave me a sense of calmness to put the angelic concept into a perspective that worked for me, at least. All in all, I found it strange—or "curiouser and curiouser"—that you had intermingled the angel into your narrative, albeit you chose one of the biggies in mentioning Michael. And so I sign off as*

> *Rafael…my real name…oh yes,*
> *the Angel of Healing*

This morning I replied that he had given me my meditation for today. I have always considered the most appealing angelic encounter in the history of art the angel Raphael appearing to the young Tobias in the Renaissance painting by Girolamo Savoldo of "Tobias and the Angel" in Rome's Borghese Gallery. It was on view at the Met last year in the "Leonardo and Lombardy" show, and I have just found a stunning reproduction of it on the Internet, which I emailed to "Rafael," adding that with his name, he really should have been an ophthalmologist, since in the Old Testament *Book of Tobit*, the angel Raphael gives Tobias the means to cure his father Tobit's blindness (cataracts). Then I recalled that our son Charlie was an angel in his first-grade Nativity play, at age six—he has not been one since. His younger brother, Chris, followed years later as the even more unlikely—and bespectacled—Virgin Mary!

A morning email from my physician/pen pal presents the challenge of facing the "historical Jesus." Faith needs to be challenged from time to time in order to mature, but it is a disturbing wake-up message on this quiet weekend morning:

> *If we accept the notions—not just put forth by Brown in* The Da Vinci Code, *but by others—that Jesus had to be gainfully employed and married so that he had credibility, then it stands to reason that he was a married carpenter. History tells us that he was a carpenter…somehow that is a safe enough profession…I care little about the novel's assertion about the Code…what I found interesting and palatable was the married and, yes, human aspect of Christ.*
>
> *Somehow I could relate better to someone like that…the one in the New Testament is unapproachable… Hey, here's your chance to get me back into the fold with solid arguments….*

My first response is that the sacred silence of unknowing what we thought we knew—call it latent agnosticism—may accompany any level of faith: there is, after all, so much beyond our ken. But the more I reflect on the good doctor's doubts and hypotheses about the historical Jesus (as distinct from the Christ of the faith), the more it seems an exercise in futility: we can never recreate the human Jesus, and the more we try, the more we risk projecting our own images onto the figure.

The four Gospels may indeed lack dispassionate objectivity, but they are nonetheless faithful portraits of a figure that transcended human outlines (in the eyes and memories of his followers). Perhaps the only question that really matters is this: Can we accept the notion that God may enter our/his world? Or, more simply, can we accept the existence of God in the first place? If the answer is no, then any other question about Jesus is a waste of time. If the answer is yes, then we may accept with faith the limits of our knowledge and our inability to fill in all the details. The living Christ of faith ultimately eclipses the human Jesus of two millennia ago.

Another email announces that the doctor's wife, who is Jewish, has asked him to accompany her and their dog to the local Episcopal Church today for a service of blessing of the animals. Is this a new twist on Francis Thompson's "hound of heaven"? God may use oblique means to reel in his strays? Who knows, I replied: you start blessing dogs and eventually you may work your way up—or down—to humans!

I got to St. Vincent's late for the noon Mass, but in time to marvel at the baskets of roses arranged at both the

---

Rosary and high altars. A special donation box "for the roses" was clue enough that something special was being celebrated—not just a wedding or funeral. I peeked in the missal while a lector read the day's Scripture: "Feast of Our Lady of the Rosary." I should have guessed, especially in a Dominican Church, whose patron saint established the practice of praying the rosary. The gospel reading today describes Jesus' passage from his earthly parents to his heavenly father, at that crucial stage of early adolescence when he leaves Mary and Joseph on their return home from Jerusalem and stays in the temple for discussions with the elders. His worried parents, upon finding him, must accept that their ties have been loosened; their son is pursuing his own destiny. It is a poignant reading for any parent. The prior's homily sounded an unsettling note, as he reminded us that this "finding Jesus in the temple" marks the last of the five "joyful mysteries" (beginning with the annunciation) and the threshold of the five "sorrowful mysteries" to follow: the agony in the garden, the scourging, the crowning with thorns, carrying the cross, and the crucifixion. After the Mass, I walked over to the Rosary altar, which I consider still my father's memorial as the tenth anniversary of his death approaches, placed a donation in the slot, and then prayed a few Hail Marys as I surveyed the brilliant assemblage of saints in their niches awaiting All Saints' Day. At the conclusion of those Hail Marys, I heard the voice of Paul McCartney from my freshman year there singing, "Let it be, let it be." Mother Mary knows best. But still I left the church with more than a renewed farewell to my dad. At the offering stand was a pile of pamphlets with rose petals and apt words to color the day:

> An illustrious and pious Dominican tells us that the rose is a perfect figure of the excellence of the Holy Rosary, and of its different mysteries. The green leaves of the rose bush represent the joyful mysteries; the thorns, the sorrowful mysteries; the flowers, the glorious mysteries. Again, the joyful, sorrowful, and glorious mysteries are brought to mind by the white, red, and yellow, or golden flowers of the rose. Rosebuds are a figure of Jesus in his infancy; the half-blown blossoms represent his passion; and the full-blown flower shows forth the glory of his triumph.

Not a bad way to mark the end of summer—and the gradual fading of our garden until next Eastertide.

This morning I receive the bill for my delight at the workings of God's hidden hand. Chris has sent me an urgent assignment:

> Dad, please help me with this intriguing topic for an analytical essay due on Saturday. I want to write about God's exceedingly limited influence, as a result of recent theological discovery (i.e., why God is less important as we progress in existential "understanding"). Some sources would be appreciated, as well as

*your opinion. I could even cite you if that's OK. Or your book.*

How to answer such a tall order? Is it really true that God's influence is "exceedingly limited"—or are our methods of measurement just inadequate?

The prevalence of unbelief is nothing new; it's all a question of how we define God. Nothing in theology or philosophical existentialism disproves God; it may, however, refine our concept of what God means. The biggest substitution since the nineteenth century has been a transference of belief/faith in God-the-miracle-worker to Science; in the past, men attributed to God the phenomena of science/medicine that they did not understand. God's chief role was to fill the gaps, a master mason more than divine architect of a universe perceived as the product of "intelligent design". But science is about the mechanics, the natural processes of existence: how things work, how they don't; it does not explain on a moral or philosophical plane their ultimate purpose or reason for being. Many of the greatest scientists—including Newton, Einstein, and my own confirmation sponsor, Sir Hugh Taylor, who discovered the chemical process essential to the atom bomb—believed in God. Man will always make a god, even if he ceases to believe in a traditional one "beyond himself": he will make a Superman (himself) the God, as the Nazis did; or the collective State (as the Soviets did); or delve into occult and New Age cults like Scientology. The best argument to be made is that as we progress in knowledge (*science* in its literal meaning), we must revise our child-like, limited preconceptions of God. As this unknown and unknowable mystery continues to unfold as backdrop, if not foreground, through the comedies and tragedies we play out on our revolving stage, we gain an increasing appreciation of our limitations, once the brilliance of godlike achievement has faded to its proper hue. Only by retaining—or regaining—humility and awe do we have any hope of avoiding the temptation—call it the devil's lure or a genetic/environmental mutation—that convinces us to make ourselves the absolute masters; that is to say, monsters.

The first pages of Chris's draft arrived early this morning, and I was awed by glimmers of brilliance. He begins,

> *With experience comes new wisdom. But in the case of God, how do we know that we are growing wiser? The question of God's existence usually precedes the equally exhausted inquiry: how do we define Him (Her, or It)? Throughout the Old Testament, God enjoyed direct judgment over humanity. In the Book of Psalms, believers learned that if they "Take delight in the Lord, / He will give [them] the desires of [their] heart[s]" (37:4). However, in 1641, René Descartes eliminated the image of a sentimental, anthropomorphic God, along with all other preordained notions of divine attributes. As he composed his Meditations, Descartes cleansed his theological palette in*

*order to determine "certain and indubitable" truths.*
*After establishing the certainty of his own existence*
*("Cogito ergo sum"), Descartes illustrated his idea of*
*God as "sovereign, eternal, infinite, immutable, all-*
*knowing, all-powerful, and the creator of all things*
*that are out of himself."*

God may indeed be immutable, but our understanding of him over the millennia is quite the opposite. In the Old Testament, he is introduced as a paternal figure displaying the full spectrum of human emotions—from anger and wrath to pity and compassion. This God might barter with Abraham over the destruction of Sodom or drown the Egyptian army in the Red Sea. In the New Testament, he is identified by Jesus as a loving father as well as a judge. Then the Christian theologians took over and added layers of Greek philosophy to the God of the patriarchs, prophets, and Jesus: from St. Augustine through Thomas Aquinas and down to the neo-Thomists of our age. Chris's paper brought back to mind those "proofs"—both ontological and cosmological—that I studied all too fleetingly my freshman year at Princeton, on the brink of conversion. Once I became a Catholic, I gave them no more thought: case closed. But Chris has reopened it, and now I must examine an unexamined faith—if only to give some hint of an explanation of where I have been all these years. I wrote back,

*I think you should acknowledge as you go on, or at the*
*end, that ultimately the existence of God, while subject*

*to reason and proofs of the intellect, is rooted in experience, not in scientific or logical proof. Descartes comes closest to this point: we cannot prove our own existence, but we can experience it. Science can describe the effects of love but cannot define or prove Love. All descriptions of God are metaphors and subject to the limitations of our language and imagination. God is, quite literally, "Beyond Proof."*

This morning Chris awakened us with a call to say that he had been up all night writing his paper and was emailing it to me to read before his class. I was amazed at the sophistication of the thought and writing, although it is clear that in this particular course—"The Challenge of Unbelief"—at his (and my old) "church school," the cards have been stacked to favor the doubting Thomases. Bishop Robinson's "death of God" theology, now forty years old, still reverberates along the corridors as much as when I was a student there. Yet Chris's concluding sentences offered some—even if ironic—glimmer of hope for faith:

> *After* Honest to God, *humanity has slowly entered a period during which it would be "archaic" to ponder over a biblical, Descartesian, or Paleyan model of God. And with Post's refutation of the PSR, it may someday seem irrational to consider any possibility of a Higher Power. Despite these somewhat troubling,*

*theory-shattering nuances toward God, people should continue to deduce their beliefs from the available evidence without fear of receiving a future stigma of ignorance. After all, doctors in medieval England could not expect Penicillin to replace blood-letting, so they continued to practice the most effective procedures of the times. If our society remains true to its collective theistic beliefs, regardless of the subordinating trend toward God's depiction, then we can establish a true marker for the progression of knowledge. However, if we are afraid to express our views because our great-great-grandchildren will someday laugh at our theological grasps, as well as our petty land-mobiles, then we neglect to use the gift of sensitive intelligence, which gives us the ability to learn from our ancestors.*

Chris allowed the door of faith to open a crack; I could not resist pushing it a bit and so added my own gloss on his conclusion. I wonder whether he might consider the proposition that those medieval doctors, despite their incorrect prescriptions, were right about the most important point: the presumed existence of a medical means of treating—and often curing—disease. We should keep seeking God even as we acknowledge that our prescriptions—age-old definitions and descriptions—have so far been proven wanting.

Maestro Mason Senft, as usual, offered via email the perfect response to the existence of God debate retraced by his former music pupil Chris:

> *I never really give much thought to the God contro-versy. If I'm ever in a spiritual crisis of faith (which is rarer than a butterfly in winter) and in need of some reaffirmation, I merely listen to "Vissi d'arte" and I know, without a moment of spiritual dalliance, that God is alive and well and living in Puccini! But it's always comforting to note there are others on alter-nate spiritual journeys who will end up at the same destination as the rest of us despite their circuitous methods.*

The email reminds me of Paul Tillich's eulogy to Martin Buber forty years ago at a memorial service here in New York. He said that we all are journeying toward the same spiritual destination by different routes. Home by another route.

This evening the gospel reading was the account of the Pharisees (the Jewish fundamentalists) and the Hero-dians (who collaborated with the Roman authorities) try-ing to trap Jesus by asking him whether it was right to pay taxes to Caesar—something a pious Jew would have considered wrong, but also something that the occupying Romans considered treason to resist. Asking them to show him a coin, Jesus in turn tricked the Pharisee into revealing that he carried a Roman coin with the emperor's image on it (something that strictly speaking was the property of the emperor and, more important, was considered improper for the pious Jew to possess). Then he uttered his famous cryptic answer: "Render unto Caesar the things that are Caesar's and to God the things that are God's." That surely pleased the Herodians, as it has every political establishment down to the present day. But the Pharisees would have caught the irony. What really belongs to God? *The whole of creation.* Everything is God's, and we owe him nothing less. That is the heart of Jesus' message. It is as impossible to fathom as a rich man passing through the eye of the needle. But with God, we are assured, everything is possible. And so we must try and, failing, try again.

Now as I approach the tenth anniversary of my dad's death, I cannot help confessing that where he worked and walked and played and worshipped hold much more evocative weight for me at this stage than the plot of earth that covers fleshless bones. Imagination is slave not to the clinical, but to the sacramental. That is why pilgrimages succeed where tourist traps fail. Imagination requires space and time through which to move; the elusive vision or memory or emotional charge rarely catches the static observer or the detached attendant. We break through time, and come back home through an act of uncalculated will. It is nothing less than a temporal consummation that sometimes splits open a crack in eternity.

The all-too-familiar gospel passage (about Jesus being asked by the Pharisees what is the greatest of the commandments) sent up an unexpected flare of new light: I had never paid attention to the obvious fact that when asked to cite the "greatest," he gives them two instead of the obvious one: "You must love the Lord your God with all your heart, soul, and mind." (It makes sense that the greatest is listed first on Moses' tablets.) But the second, "like unto it," that we must love our neighbors as ourselves is nowhere to be found among the Ten received from the peak of Mount Sinai. Rather, Jesus distills it from a passage in the Book of Leviticus. And he gives it a new twist with the New Testament revision of what a "neighbor" is (a question answered by the parable of the Good Samaritan). He gives his listeners more to ponder than they had sought. He is more than Moses, who nonetheless will take second place to stand at his side during the transfiguration.

Today we watched the Breeder's Cup races—not at Belmont, but on television. I could not have stood the tension of being physically present. My English cousin Jonathan Pease, the trainer of Bago, favored by many to win its turf race, had too much at stake. His immediate family had crossed the Atlantic to join him, but they were seasoned race goers. The wet weather had left the turf soft, and Bago does not like a soft course. I feared that weather, that uncontrollable variable, might prove the champion-maker and heartbreaker. I offered a brief prayer for Bago, but I could not ask God to help him win. Why? I am still struggling with the notion of intercession, praying for favors from a personal God, even if the favors are for others. It does not seem worthy of God. That's what I tell myself. But is that really the reason? Or is it that I want to insulate myself from disappointment, the rejection of a petition? I must think more about how personal our God-beyond-gods may be. In the meantime, Bago ran an elegant race; he finished fourth.

Late last night, after watching *Dial M for Murder* for the first time in its original color, I turned to Greeley's prayer journal and read, by divine coincidence, his musings on whether God suffered with, for, or because of us, his creatures. He notes that while theologians such as Küng deem the notion of a suffering God—literally a compassionate God—unworthy of absolute divinity, the witness of the Old Testament prophets testifies otherwise. This question really strikes at the heart of the personal God question. Can God be deliberately self-limiting in order to suffer with his creation? Is that choice really a limitation, a self-imposed boundary on the infinite? Or are we, in our most modern and secular sophistication, the ones who are self-limiting in formulating a God who would not encompass our deepest, most humanizing emotions raised to an infinite plane: love, compassion, pity, sorrow? The priest at St. Gertrude's today—he was from the Philippines and hardly seemed older than a schoolboy—marveled at our celebration of Halloween here, only two days away: in America, it ranks second only to Christmas. It steals the show from the next day, the Feast of All Saints, just as Dante's *Inferno* eclipses *Paradiso*. Of course our neo-pagan Halloween is lighthearted: its ghosts, goblins, devils, and demons are sugarcoated with humor. All in good fun. Nothing serious—anymore than Santa's troubles with reindeer. But on a church bulletin board I read a timely saying of Reinhold Niebuhr: "Humor is a prelude to faith and laughter is the beginning of prayer." Perhaps the universe is, after all, a Divine Comedy. What then are we to make of God?

Here on Halloween I finally cannot stand the constant distraction from the Mass as I look upward at the rood and try to decipher the rest of the dimly-lit Latin inscription. The inscription over the pulpit is more visible, but equally unfamiliar. Afterward I go back to the sacristy and ask Father Jones whether he can solve the riddle of these two inscriptions. He tells me they are both from St. Paul. The one over the pulpit (*Praedica verbum; insta opportune, importune; argue, obsecra, increpa in omni patientia et doctrina.*) is from Paul's Second Letter to Timothy, in which he charges him to "Preach the word! Be ready in season and out of season. Convince, rebuke, exhort, with all longsuffering and teaching"—apt words to gild over a pulpit in a Dominican Church manned by that "order of preachers." The rood inscription, he told me, is from Paul's Letter to the

Galatians. I went home to look it up, in both the Vulgate and English editions, but I could not find a match for the words I had already deciphered. Toward the end of the epistle, Paul writes, "But God forbid that I should glory except in the cross of our Lord Jesus Christ, by whom the world has been crucified to me, and I to the world" (6:14). Yet our inscription is communal, not singular: it begins with "nos" (we). And it concludes with the words for salvation, life, and resurrection. I went to Google, the closest yet to the mind of God; here, too, no match for this particular phrase was to be found anywhere in the Bible. But Google did not fail me. It directed me first to an obscure medieval manuscript, then to the *Missale Romanum*, where the mystery was solved as I read: *Nos autem gloriari oportet in cruce Domini nostri Jesu Christi, in quo est salus, vita, et resurrectio nostra*—the very words on the rood, taken from the Introit for the Feast of the Invention (meaning Discovery) of the True Cross ("But it befits us to glory in the cross of our Lord Jesus Christ, in whom is our salvation, life, and resurrection"). I also, as an added dividend, found a reference to a musical setting of this text by the great Palestrina. So what has begun as a Halloween adventure in biblical sleuthing may end in a feast for the ears.

This morning I listened to a sampling of the Palestrina "*Nos Autem Gloriari*" via the Internet; it was hard to make out the Latin text through the layers of Renaissance polyphony.

But I also found a version in Gregorian chant, as clear as spring water. I can now understand why the Church a century ago wanted to return to this chant for sung Masses—but not out of any special veneration of the Middle Ages. In the ears of Mother Church, words take precedence over notes, text over music. I can understand the reasoning, but still I believe that the angels—like so many mortals—prefer Mozart.

Driving along an interstate highway, through a passage of shadows worthy of Dante, I recalled that prayer of so many Graham Greene characters: take away what is most precious to me, even my life itself, in return for sparing my loved one. In the real world, unlike "Greeneland," God does not barter; yet we mortal creatures, in life as in fiction, always revert to it in times of duress. By the time I left the remains of daylight and entered St. Vincent Ferrer for the evening Mass, I thought of a better prayer, one that God surely answers: that charity—God's overwhelming love—may prevail over all odds and obstacles. I have a small book, *The Spiritual Vision of Pope Benedict XVI: Let God's Light Shine Forth*, that my editor sent to me several months ago. Two of Benedict's observations strike me as illuminating not only God, but also the mystery of pain. The first:

> *Love is always a kind of death. We die again and again in marriage, in the family, and in all our dealings with fellow men. The power of selfishness can be explained*

*in the light of this experience. It is a flight—an all too understandable flight—from the mystery of death that is love. At the same time, however, it is only this death that is love which is really fruitful.*

The second:

*Pain is part of being human. Anyone who really wanted to get rid of suffering would have to get rid of love before anything else, because there can be no love without suffering, because it always demands an element of self-sacrifice, because, given temperamental differences and the drama of situations, it will always bring with it renunciation and pain....Anyone who has inwardly accepted suffering becomes more mature and more understanding of others, becomes more human.*

As to the great philosophical *Why*—why must life be so, why didn't a God who is Love craft us with perfection in lieu of pain?—well, we have no answer, just God's own example in Jesus, that is to say, himself. Our Christian faith has never promised an immediate answer, just a path to follow: the footsteps of Jesus.

I love today's Feast of Christ the King. I'm not sure why. Is it because it marks the end of Ordinary Time, sounding a royal note of triumph before the penitential season of

Advent, the days of waiting and expectation leading to the lights of Christmas? Or because I associate it with the height of fall and the Thanksgiving feast? It meant nothing to me as a child; it didn't exist for me until my sophomore year at Princeton, my first term as a newly minted Catholic. There in the University Chapel I discovered it thanks to a rousing sermon preached by Archbishop Fulton J. Sheen, who thundered, "Christ the King rules from a cross."

Today, thirty-five years later, I entered the little church of St. John the Martyr to find it decorated in fall foliage at the altar. Fall is my favorite season, ablaze with the colors of an earthbound sunset before the night of winter. And the King I encountered there was a different one: the Good Shepherd who tends his flock, the shepherd-king who, in the words of the hymnist, is above all the "king of Love." That was the very king I needed today marking the last Sunday of Ordinary Time. May this King of Love rule all our hearts. May he give us—or make of us—a Christopher, a "bearer of Christ."

This morning I went with Ritchie to the Met to visit the Prague show with her. I would not have gone on my own, and that would have been a mistake. The exhibit is of stunning, mostly religious artifacts from the late Middle Ages and early Renaissance. I know so little about that gem of a city, which I largely associate with Mozart—his Prague symphony and the premiere of *Don Giovanni*. There were several revelations: I didn't know that Charlemagne, the first Holy Roman Emperor, had been canonized—St. Charlemagne! (Perhaps I should adopt him as my name saint?) I suspect that St. Charles Borromeo has a better claim to sanctity. Then I discovered the Emperor Charles IV, who moved the capital of his empire to Prague. I must encourage my son of that numeral to visit this show. In the end, it was more the sense of place and time that left the deepest imprint, not the individual artworks, although the reliquaries and monstrances were second to none.

Perhaps it was the afterglow of that contemporary exhibit that prompted me to go to the postmodern church of St. Hyacinth for the Saturday vigil Mass on Long Island. It is the local Polish church, and as soon as I entered the brightly lit interior with white marble and gleaming blue mosaics, I thought of the late pope. There is nothing sublime or mysterious about this sanctuary, just spotlights of affirmation and joy. The crucifix is overshadowed by the promise of resurrection, a suitable message for this first Sunday in Advent. St. Hyacinth is the parish church of Mason Senft, whom Chris and I claim in common as music coach and inspiration. I was hoping to see him there, but it is enough to know that he worships in the same space, and partakes of the same sacrament.

# ADVENT

The last day of the month: tomorrow I get to open the first window of my Advent calendar. A call to Dame Elisabeth confirmed that she is recovering from eye surgery and will attend her ninetieth birthday concert next week but that she would rather I visit next month when we may have more private time together. I told her that that seemed much better to me since I really want to do her justice in the celebratory piece I shall write for *Opera News*. I am relieved not to travel abroad while son Chris is out in the Utah desert for a wilderness retreat; she sounded equally grateful for the schedule change. I must leave my calendar to God more often.

I entered St. Vincent to the sound of the Gloria being recited. What, I wondered, is the special occasion? It turns out that today is the Feast of St. Andrew, the first of the disciples to be called—a fisherman called to become "a fisher of men." I thought of Father Andrew, an expert fisher of young souls, and then of my two favorite Baroque churches in Rome, both dedicated to this saint: Sant' Andrea della Valle, the setting of the first act of *Tosca*, and Bernini's Sant'

Andrea al Quirinale, that oval gem—an opera in stone, stucco, gilt, paint, light, and space—which the old maestro said was the work that "displeased him least." Until today I have thought of Andrew mostly by his end on the cross; now I must think first of his calling. We are still called to be fishers for the kingdom. As I write these words, WQXR has just announced and has begun to play a selection from Strauss's operetta "A Night in Venice" starring Elisabeth Schwarzkopf! I wish I could claim authorship of such divine coincidences, but I cannot. That is why I cannot trade fact for fiction. The former is so much more exquisite—and mysterious.

Today I finally completed a shopping assignment that has been looming for over a week and that I started tackling this past weekend. It was spelled out on a card I had picked from the "giving tree" beside the altar at St. John the Martyr: "Personal items for a homeless man." The list included deodorant, soap, a comb and brush, toothbrush and toothpaste, razor and shaving cream, and something less obvious: "sweet socks." Everything except that last item I found in the course of weekly shopping at the supermarket. It had been a daunting list at first, but once I started, I found myself in a child's treasure hunt along aisle two. Then this morning the editor within took charge and I recognized the last puzzling item for what it was—a misprint. I had wondered whether sweet socks were something like Granny Glittens's amazing mittens from one of my favorite childhood stories in *The Tall*

*Book of Christmas*, mittens that she had dyed with solutions of lemon drops, wintergreen, licorice, and the like. They were good enough to eat—and that is precisely what the happy recipients did with them. But in this case, the answer was more prosaic, a misplaced letter. As I procrastinated, I wished for a simpler solution to Christmas charity: writing a check would have been so much easier. But now that the assignment is done, the items—capped by sweat socks—all fitted snugly into a small gift bag, I can appreciate the wisdom of Father Baker, who sets up his giving tree each year in the church. The very process of shopping not only personalizes the gift—basic items we all take for granted—but *sacramentalizes* it. Each of the objects has a tangible quality that evokes the act of self-care associated with it. Each is a small physical reminder of the greater plight of the homeless and needy during this annual feast of conspicuous consumption. Many have less than even a warm stable on that holy night, and no kings will come from afar bearing precious gifts to them. Now that I have filled my one small bag, I wonder why I did not think to buy in triplicate. But, as Jesus foretold at the end of his life, we shall always have the poor with us—and not just at Christmas.

At the noon Mass, I discovered today's Feast of St. John of the Cross, best known for his vivid account of his "dark night of the soul." I recall so little else about this Counter-Reformation Spanish mystic, but Father Carlton piqued my curiosity by explaining in his homily that John considered devotion to the cross the privileged path to the resurrection. Afterward, in the sacristy, he showed me a canticle by this poet-saint in which he writes that "it is quite impossible to reach the thicket of the riches and wisdom of God except by first entering the thicket of much suffering, in such a way that the soul finds there its consolation and desire. The soul that longs for divine wisdom chooses first, and in truth, to enter the thicket of the cross." Both treasure and redemption, it seems, are surrounded, like the blooming rose, by thorns.

The crèche at St. Vincent's is now peopled; the animals outnumber the humans two to one (not counting the two angels since they fit neither slot). No wonder my two-year-old Charlie, once upon a time, burst into song when he first confronted this stable scene: "Ee—eye—ee—eye—oh!" Only the Christ Child remains to be added on Christmas Eve, joined later by those three magnificent Magi with their retinue.

A mile north, I revisited another Epiphany: the stained glass window behind the high altar of St. Thomas More, my first Catholic parish here in New York. I was in the area doing some late Christmas shopping and decided to step inside for old time's sake. I almost did not, for I saw a sign posted on the church door directing visitors to the parish house. But then a homeless man, laden with shopping bags, opened the door from the inside and held it for me. The only other soul inside was another man sleeping on a pew. I made my way to the front and sat in what once was our family pew. Our children are grown and dispersed. But in vivid color, especially in late afternoon, the Holy Family remains unchanged, the Christ Child forever new. I look forward to Epiphany.

I have ended Christmas Eve as always, for the past many years, by replaying a tape of Francis Robinson's radio broadcast "A Collector's Christmas." He died a quarter century ago. New York lost "Mr. Metropolitan Opera" and I lost a mentor and friend. But his inimitable Tennessee baritone resounds over the loudspeakers again as he fills the room with his wonder and love of music to capture the spirit of Christmas. I am back again in my twenties, if only for an hour before the chime of midnight strikes, as the spirit of Christmas present dissolves the mirage of Christmas past.

# CHRISTMAS

Early this morning, before going off to bed, I watched the conclusions of two midnight Masses—Pope Benedict's at St. Peter's and Cardinal Egan's at St. Patrick's. Thanks to the remote control, I was able to cross back and forth the Atlantic several times a minute, as witness to both holy sacrifices. In the end, Rome won—no surprise. St. Pat's has a fine Gothic baldachin—but it's not Bernini's.

Today the Feast of the Holy Innocents finds us in Florida. The young priest at St. Christopher's seemed a holy innocent himself as he informed us that the size of Bethlehem at the time of Christ's birth meant the number of infants and toddlers murdered by Herod would have ranged between twenty and twenty-five. It sounded close enough to the number—not that I've ever counted them—in Rubens's record-breaking painting. His *Massacre of the Innocents* had hung in an Austrian monastery before it was sold at auction a few years ago to Lord Thomson, the newspaper baron, for the highest price ever paid for an old master painting. It is as stunning a tour de force of brushwork and color as it is unbearable a subject. Of course, as the young priest observed, the massacre of innocents continues on a far greater scale two thousand years after Herod's purge. But then he added a new insight: the innocents are no longer limited to young children. All baptized souls are newborn innocents, as we are so rendered anew each time we emerge from a confessional, cleansed by absolution. No innocents, he concluded, deserve a death sentence; nor perhaps do the guilty, he added. That jolt of Catholic teaching at its best—especially here in a state that sponsors capital punishment—casts this strange feast in a new light. Crazed King Herod was striking a blow in Bethlehem for his survival as King of the Jews—self-defense, he might have argued. Can we claim as much?

Last night son Charlie raised the question of prayer—not a typical after-dinner topic of discussion. Now that he is an Alabamian as well as Episcopalian, he goes to church every Sunday and says grace at family meals with his future in-laws. He said he also prayed each night, but confessed that he finds it more natural to pray for self-improvement than for others or for favors. The notion of intercession is difficult to grasp. Why do we pray for others, for victims, for peace? The only answer I can offer is that it is an acknowledgment of our human limitations, our inborn need for God. We alone cannot solve every crisis, though we should never stop trying. Charlie asks whether the Bible records any examples of granted prayers. I said I was sure it does although I could not think of any specific examples. It is easier to cite examples of Jesus performing miracles.

Perhaps prayer transforms the petitioner internally more often than it affects the external world. We pray because we need to pray. And every such prayer should include a thanksgiving—the one prayer that never needs, or seeks, an answer.

# EPIPHANY

The Feast of Epiphany. As soon as I entered St. Thomas Episcopal Church on Fifth Avenue, I realized that its famous choir school was still on vacation; the only choristers in the stalls were a dozen men. The crèche in the center of the sanctuary was similarly edited: accompanying Mary, Joseph, and the Baby Jesus were only the Three Kings—no shepherds or animals. At St. Thomas, this feast belongs to the royal Gentiles. But, to be fair, both Scripture and Tradition suggest that the Three Magi arrived long after the shepherds on that first Christmas night—perhaps as long as two years after. And the homilist made the point that this feast signifies the extension of the Messiah's realm to include the Gentiles; in other words, the universality of redemption: Christ came to save the world, nothing less. After the service had concluded, I walked up to the right transept, near the pulpit, where a poignant corpus hung on a cross, built into the massive pier, made of stones from Mount Calvary. The corpus, which transformed that cross into a crucifix, had been given in memory of our dear friend David Alger, who perished in the Towers on 9/11. It had been dedicated by the Archbishop of Canterbury and, below, its memorial inscription was composed by the Queen—a masterpiece of Christian distillation: "Grief is the price we pay for love." The days leading up to this Epiphany have been personally painful ones, days of grief. The poet Eliot had one of the Three Kings describe his experience of his visit to the Christ Child as a kind of death. An old order had died at Bethlehem; renewal and redemption are born through death, just as baptism signifies both death and rebirth. Last Epiphany marked the beginning of a journey that would come full circle. May this one signal the setting out for our true home—by another route.

# Epilogue

## A Pilgrimage to Schruns:
## Elisabeth Schwarzkopf at Ninety

This morning I landed in Paris en route to Zürich, the first airborne leg of my pilgrimage to Schruns in Vorarlberg, Austria, to visit Dame Elisabeth Schwarzkopf. She has lived in Schruns these past three years, under a glistening tiara of snowcapped Alps, ever since moving from her house in Zumikon, outside Zürich. I had hoped to time my visit to celebrate her ninetieth birthday last month, but a family obligation drew me westward to the Rockies when I wanted to soar like Strauss orchestrations through the Alps.

So now I finally arrive on the heels of Mozart's 250th birthday, his *bicenquinquagenary*, a term I discovered at a Princeton celebration a decade ago. Mozart was born in the year that Nassau Hall—the center of the Princeton campus—was completed.

I am sitting in an old inn called the Hemingway beside the village church of St. Jodok, so refreshing in its sorbet hues and beckoning with its confectionery onion dome atop the bell tower. It's a blessedly short stroll through snowy streets to my hotel, the Zimba, a few houses down from

Schwarzkopf's flat on the Veltlinerweg. It's all within a stone's throw of the train station, where I was thrilled to arrive at the end of the Montafonerbahn.

Back home, I had boasted that getting here would take two planes and four trains. I had miscalculated: the total of trains numbered six—a daunting itinerary to decipher. But I made it—one train at a time, and lots of frantic interviews in between. When in early stages of apprehension I reached Elisabeth via cell phone, I confessed that I felt like Tannhäuser setting off on his Roman pilgrimage.

She directed me to raise my sights and look up at the mountains—pitch-perfect advice. Our Rockies cannot compete; these Alps take the gold. As the train passed alongside a lake outside Zürich, the fine mist rising from frigid water cast the magnificent mountain backdrop in a gray-slate haze, a Romantic veil that mirrored a Caspar David Friedrich landscape. Oscar Wilde was right: art doesn't imitate nature; nature imitates art.

I have never written more than a postcard in a restaurant. But Hemingway's has a long wooden table with no one else at it; I might as well be sitting at my desk back home while two neighboring tables of cheerful Austrian skiers provide a steady current of melodic conversation strong enough to ward off my self-consciousness. The waitress stops and comments that I "write very fast." So perhaps enough self-consciousness has remained to recast me as a student dying to finish his homework before being called out for sacrilege in a tavern.

But then I recall that my family's most Ernest author

used to write in cafés and in fact came to Schruns with his wife Hadley and infant son, and stayed a full six months, long enough to complete his first great novel, *The Sun Also Rises*, an idyllic interlude he later chronicled at the end of *A Moveable Feast*.

I was reminded of that literary footnote as I boarded my fourth train—from Buchs to Feldkirch—which would transport me from Switzerland, through Liechtenstein, and finally across the border into Austria. Its side was emblazoned *The Ernest Hemingway*; I knew at last I was on the right track. Hemingway's centennial had illustrated the fruits of his favorite maxim, *Il faut (d'abord) durer*: he has endured.

But today that footnote belongs to the impeccable Dame Elisabeth: at ninety she has justly been hailed the greatest singer of Mozart for the second half of the past century, certainly for my lifetime and arguably her own as well. That is my thesis to be inked and underscored on the pristine cream-colored pages of this leather-bound journal that my bride, Ritchie, gave me as a wedding gift more than twenty-six years ago. Its gold-stamped year, 1979, was as sad for Elizabeth as it was happy for me. That was the year her husband, Walter Legge, died just three days after her farewell concert, at the close of which he had proclaimed her "a bloody miracle." Through my five decades of listening, she has projected into sound the absolute ideal of beauty—what Shakespeare called "the constant image."

Tonight, a few minutes before my arrival, Elisabeth called the Hotel Zimba and ordered a bottle of wine for me. The young woman at the desk spoke hardly a word of

English as she tried to explain that "Professor Dr. Schwarzkopf" had sent a bottle of wine to my room as a welcome gift. The only words that came to my mind were Oktavian's (disguised as the maid Mariandl) in the last act of *Der Rosenkavalier*: *"Nein, nein, nein, nein, I trink'kein Wein."* No problem: they happily exchanged it for a bottle of mineral water!

I am to stop by her house tomorrow at eleven thirty, for our first face-to-face visit in two decades. I shall try to do her justice, as I promised, on the subject of Mozart. She and Mozart inhabit special niches in my pantheon of music: all air and light. *"Dove sono i bei momenti?"*

Sitting almost alone in the breakfast room of the Zimba, while most of the families have already taken to the slopes, I can see through the lightly draped picture windows the Alps and patches of the clearest blue skies I can recall. I am sure I have seen as blue in Maine or even Florida, but here the backdrop of the Alps and the reflections of the snowcapped peaks work their morning magic—and long beyond first light.

I have almost two hours until I walk over to Elisabeth's. Time to meander in daylight and daydream about an excursion up the mountains. I worried last night about how I would pass the time when Elisabeth was not free to discuss Mozart. In the clear light of day, such worries are soon dispelled.

The church of St. Jodok is magnificent, a polychrome

Baroque feast of woodcarving. There was no Mass this morning, but somehow the space, so freezing that a sheet of ice covered the font of holy water, seemed even more suited to a votive candle at the Virgin's altar. I was able to make out enough of the German prayer to leave my flickering candle as a silent sacrament to light the rest of the day. And so it did.

I still cannot believe that it has been twenty years since I last saw Elisabeth Schwarzkopf, whom I first met in 1981, the year my father published *On and Off the Record*, her memoir and collection of writings by her recently deceased husband, Walter Legge, the legendary record producer at EMI and arguably the past century's most influential impresario in classical music.

I had escorted her around a maze of publishers at the Frankfurt Book Fair that fall and later, as my reward, attended her master classes over the next three years at the Mannes College of Music in my hometown, New York. Fifteen years later, in 2000, we renewed a friendship via phone and fax, prompted by my arranging for a reissue of the book, for which I had the enviable assignment of choosing photographs from her collection, composing her captions in the first person (the ultimate reward for an accidental life in publishing), and thereby retracing vicariously her luminous career.

This morning, as she greets me at her door, two decades vanished in an *Augenblick*: her face shines with expression, her eyes sparkle with wit and warmth, and her voice rings as clear in speech as on record. She directs me into her music room, awash in pale winter light. Though February is still a day away, we are surrounded by flowers in full bloom, a collage of color photographs she took of the gardens her husband planted for her over the years, to welcome her home from world-ranging tours of concert and opera stages. We are seated on an eighteenth-century love seat for most of our first two-hour session; in front of us, on a delicate table beside my recording equipment, is a tray of coffee and sweets; I cannot help thinking of *Der Rosenkavalier*, act one, *sans* libretto.

"Don't you want any cream?"

"No thanks—tell me when to stop," I reply, adding a touch to her cup (recalling that Hemingway used to request from my Dad "just enough to change the color.")

"More cream, please—it is not yet forbidden."

Dominating the room is a grand piano, closed, but with a vocal score on top; at the side, by the picture window, a brass music stand displays a framed photograph of Legge; another, still larger, portrait of her late husband hangs on the far wall, directly facing—appraising?—the would-be pianist.

I confess to Elisabeth my early obsession with Mozart; as a boy pianist, I could readily identify with Schroeder in *Peanuts*, except that the bust on my piano was of Wolfgang, not Ludwig. I used to commute back and forth from piano bench to phonograph, to listen and then try to imitate Walter Gieseking playing the simplest minuets (on a classic recording of all Mozart's piano music collected aptly on Angel Records and produced by—who else?—her husband, Walter Legge).

"At least they seemed simple," she interjects. "...Ah,

Gieseking! Do you know that Gieseking, when he accompanied me on that record of Mozart lieder, never used the pedal once? That was really something unheard of—and it was perfect."

The mention of the first pianist I ever heard strikes a welcome chord.

"We do have to learn not to sing like the piano," she continues, "which is not a legato instrument—and it is very difficult because it is the instrument that most singers hear accompanying them. Pianists use the pedal to make it seem legato, but Gieseking didn't: he didn't touch the pedal at all; he just played and it sounded legato."

I am still thinking of Wolfgang, the child prodigy, and his family life in Salzburg. I ask what she thinks about the possibility of a musical gene running through families.

"Not gene," she insists, "I'd rather use the word instinct."

I ask about her parents; which of them passed on that instinct to her?

"My father took his guitar with him when he went off to fight in the First World War. He was very musical and he made me learn the guitar immediately." Then, all of a sudden, we are back to time present:

"Why did you travel so far to see me? I can't give you a performance."

"You give me a performance every day through your recordings."

"I haven't listened to a single record in this room for three years—I started one, but the acoustics were so wrong that I finished it in two minutes and never heard another.

All the CDs I have heard are a terror, not the right sound, you know; and we have lived for the sound, *lived* for the sound—and that sound was not to take us to the heights of heaven but to bring out the composer's work in the best possible manner."

I am aware of how important visualization has been in Schwarzkopf's artistry—she often called herself an *Augenmensch* [visual person]—which has long fascinated me as an art historian. When coaching Bach's *St. Matthew Passion*, for instance, she would have a student picture the famous crucifixion by Grünewald. She delighted especially in the landscapes of Monet—those "visible blessings of the past," as she once described them to me. But visualization was not only an internal process in crafting hues of color and light. The scene has to fit the notes.

"Is Mozart ideal training for young singers?" I wonder. "Can young singers perhaps harm themselves by singing too much Mozart too soon?" Here she is far more reassuring.

"No, Mozart is the ideal schooling for singers—but in the style of Mozart, not of Verdi or Wagner. The fixed style of Mozartean singing has rules, things you must do and things you must on no account do."

It comes as no surprise to a Schwarzkopf fan that her touchstone is *legato*, that quality of seamless singing in which she is peerless.

"You don't learn it through the piano, but through stringed instruments....I played the viola—not very well, but at least I had to play it. The ear is your most important instrument in making music; the ear will tell you, 'Well, that wasn't legato, that note was finished too soon, why don't I bind it, why can't I sing it in one strength out, why don't I sing as it is written in a diminuendo and then go pianissimo to the next note, legato, or sing it with a crescendo and go to a legato even in a *subito piano* after a crescendo?' All those things have to be learned via the ear, your own ear.

"Likewise, the singer has to put the right person into the sound—not your person, but the person that Mozart wanted to hear. It shouldn't just sound like Miss Schwarzkopf! The Cherubino voice is different from the Susanna voice—they are all different—and you have to have so many different voices in your voice if possible—and it is not always possible—so they may still recognize me as Schwarzkopf but they should also recognize today, 'Aha, that is Susanna!' or the next day, 'Aha, that is the Countess!'—the same opera, but different ways of singing.

"This is what you have to learn in the *Hochschule* or with a teacher or with your own *Fantasie*, your own imagination. Imagination is the means of translating into your singing a feeling of what art is and what a great composer is. You cannot sing one piece like the next."

Throughout her career she deliberately limited her roles—in some, she said, "the sound was not right for me" and in singing "you must do justice to the persona in Mozart's cast." One role that fit like a glove, a velvet one at that, was the Countess in *Figaro*. She remains, for me, the definitive Contessa.

"It was Furtwängler who most influenced me, with the sound, with the expression you must feel the second before the note. When you talk, you alter your expression every second, every part of a second; you should do that when you sing."

"So, then, no matter how carefully crafted a performance, there is always the element of the almost instantaneous?"

"Certainly."

The recording I have listened to more times than I can count, ever since I studied it for a term as a college student, is the Giulini *Figaro*, recorded after she had been singing the Countess for more than a decade. It was that conductor's first recording of a Mozart opera for Legge at EMI.

"Walter believed in him very much; I liked him very much....We all know he fought great battles inside himself to make it right, you see, to find the expression; you could feel it—that he was giving his utmost to do the right thing and never felt safe that it was the right sound; he battled for it all the time, and that brings forth great expression from a human being."

Hence the visceral excitement of a recording that has never staled in its infinite variety over decades of listening.

Speaking of battles, what about *Don Giovanni*? I read recently that whenever Schwarzkopf sang another of her signature roles, the opera might as well have been retitled *Donna Elvira*! "Elvira is the most dramatic role you can do—though Donna Anna needs a bigger voice." Did she ever sing Donna Anna?

"The arias, yes, but not the role—no, I was really

formed for Donna Elvira, I believe, because I did find—I did feel—the right expression."

But Schwarzkopf's Elvira was so magnetic, so attractive—how could the Don have ever ditched her? She once tried to fight nature and make herself repulsive.

"I put on a false nose and face and made her a very cruel looking person but it didn't work at all. Besides, if you cannot make the vocal character clear to the audience without showing her, there would be no phonograph records."

My favorite photograph from the archives, on the other hand, is a masterpiece of *chiaroscuro*—her blond Elvira opposite Leontyne Price's Donna Anna at Salzburg; my confession evokes a smile of happy memory.

"Ah, her voice was unusually beautiful, she had great expression—it's a totally different voice from mine, totally different character—and very, very good singing; there was not a flaw, never any kind of thinking back to singing Verdi or Puccini; she sang pure Mozart. She had the brains and the taste of a great artist. It was stylistically perfect."

To what should this be credited, I wonder?

"Talent, number one. Instinct, number two. Then training is utmost." What of cultural background?

"Irrelevant. I have a young Japanese singer here who sings with utmost stylistic perfection already."

So does she actually think that our European heritage will move eastward?

"Absolutely. They learn so fast—the Japanese, Chinese, and Korean singers—the minute you tell them something, they do it. It is quite incredible. I have never experienced anything like it. And the tradition will pass from Europe to these other countries."

I can't repress a certain wistfulness, Eurocentric that I am. Schwarzkopf, however, has no such qualms.

"Not at all—because the tradition will *live*!"

"Is it because there they are more respectful of our tradition?"

"Not only more respectful, but talented! They have the will—and the understanding—to produce the right sound, and not just the sound but the feeling."

I reminisce about my first trip to the Frankfurt Book Fair and Wiesbaden, where I attended a performance of *Così* in a truly cozy house, an ideal intimate staging. "I did *Don Giovanni* there," Elisabeth recalls with special warmth. She had helped settle her parents in that delightful eighteenth-century spa town for their twilight years.

"Is Mozart, then, better suited to smaller houses?"

"Yes, of course, because the discussion—the recitative—in Mozart is very fast, and passes by so quickly, and is so important for details of expression; it gets lost in a huge space."

How then did Schwarzkopf come to learn a Viennese style of singing Mozart?

"Well, I had two years of singing in Vienna's Theater an der Wien. Many of the roles I had to learn overnight, so I really learned the Vienna style of singing in those two years. But I also had a year out in the sanitarium in the Tatra Mountains of Slovakia, recovering from tuberculosis, and I took all my music with me and spent that year lying in the

woods memorizing all the parts I wanted to sing—not singing, just memorizing."

"Not every singer, I venture, would make such an
investment from such a setback."

"I think it was pure instinct."

Her teacher, Maria Ivogün, had helped make the
arrangements; across the room, her smiling picture faces us
atop the bookshelf, flanked by two deep cobalt vases. I mistake the photo of Ivogün for young Elisabeth: beauty plays
such tricks.

"Schmitt-Walter took me to her when I was a beginner
at the Berlin Opera. I was already two years at the opera
house, but Maria told me I had no technique, and we started
with two notes; for four months we did nothing but those
two notes, and then slowly we went up bit by bit, for two
years."

What about Ivogün's husband, pianist Michael
Raucheisen, with whom Schwarzkopf performed her first
lieder recitals?

"He was the most wonderful accompanist in all the
world, the greatest accompanist that ever was—*punto,
finito.*"

I want to turn the clock back even further—to the
earliest years of study; we had both attended all-boys
schools—an ocean and era apart. Hers was due to the fact
that her father was headmaster. There she learned to play a
host of instruments, from the lute and *Glockenspiel*, to the
organ (though her feet could not reach the pedals), and she
sang Mary in Christmas pageants.

Years later, progressing through Mozart roles at the Deutsche Oper, she began with Blondchen in *Die Entführung*, and then Konstanze. In *Die Zauberflöte* she started in the chorus—for the famous Beecham recording produced by her future husband, Walter Legge, in 1937—then sang one of the three boys, and finally Pamina. In *Figaro*, she passed through Barbarina to Susanna and finally the Countess, the role she owned for the rest of her career. "Which Mozart role remains the most dramatically and vocally challenging?"

"Even the slightest folk song is challenging all the time. But I would have to say Fiordiligi, which is very long and very hard to sing well. You have to hold a true position of your voice throughout, and you really don't even have a minute to go to your dressing room!"

It is now time to pretend—in the spirit of Walter Mitty—that I am her student. "What is the most important thing for a student of Mozart?"

"The timbre of the voice, the sound of the voice—it has to be an utterly beautiful sound, and not just the notes as such. That sound will vary from the *secco* recitatives, to the accompanied ones, to the first notes at the beginning of the aria, which is again not quite the sound of the aria itself, and so on."

"After all the preparation, at the moment of singing an aria, can a singer allow herself to enjoy the emotion, of joy, sorrow, whatever, that is being conveyed to the audience?"

"No, you must be able to put your feeling into the sound and to hear what you are doing; the ear is all important."

"What of the current vogue of spontaneity, of just being yourself?"

"No, because there is the matter of style, and the style is in the music—and if Mozart hasn't got style I don't know who has—and that style needs observation, it needs knowledge, it needs hearing, what you are doing wrong, a feeling for the tempo, for changing of color, as permitted: you don't have a lot of freedom in Mozart, but you don't have to be afraid of giving beauty to Mozart if it is true to style….and you must always obey the conductor, because Mozart is not conducted by nitwits!"

The theologian Karl Barth once quipped that in heaven Bach was court composer but that every afternoon the angels sneaked off to play Mozart. I want to know Elisabeth's appraisal of that court composer since I have long been addicted to her early recordings of his cantatas, spun with a young voice of pure silver.

Bach, she replies, is "fiendishly difficult to sing—I'd rather five times Mozart than one-half time Bach!"

Then I ask the question to which I am convinced I already have the answer: What composer, if she were allowed only one, would she keep for herself?

"Smetana."

I should know better than to second-guess Schwarzkopf. Why Smetana? His "richly loving folk sound," she replies. Not so much the vocal music as his orchestral music. Her father had loved Smetana, and so does she. Even with no roots in Czech soil, she finds listening to that composer "always a kind of homecoming."

I am determined to salvage Mozart. "Surely he was the most gifted, the most ingenious of composers?"

"I don't know. I think he is the most feared to do justice to, because not doing so is immediately audible, immediately exposed."

"Why? Isn't Bach technically as difficult?"

"More difficult, but Bach does not touch you in the same way as Mozart does. Mozart is so simple, touching you immediately with just a few notes. Bach needs many more notes to touch you."

After Dame Elisabeth enumerates the grueling details of traveling, packing, unpacking, doctors, and everything that precedes performing on tour, I ask her to pretend I am now her agent and asking her preference: a staged opera, opera in concert, or a recording?

She recalls fondly those concert performances of Mozart operas arranged by her husband in London's Festival Hall.

"You don't act across the stage but you do react to each other. I think those are the ideal performances because you don't have to concentrate on whether that chair will break down, or whether I have the right dress, but can concentrate on singing. Those were the very best opera concerts I ever did."

"I am surprised to hear this from someone as gifted in acting as in singing."

"But, you know, you can still act while standing still. You can look and listen and react to what your partners are singing. More is not needed. In the recording studio, on the other hand, one does not have the freedom even to turn and look to the side but must stand completely still and focus on the score."

At two o'clock—or is it closer to three?—it is clearly time for a break and Elisabeth encourages me to go to the top of the Hochjoch for a late lunch and for a loftier view from the mountains she has loved all her life. So I take the cable car to the top of the Hochjoch. Everyone else has skis; I have my camera. I have been deathly afraid of heights all my life, but today there is no turning back. I hope the film develops; the views are breathtaking.

When I take the cable car back down, I suddenly see that I am returning to late afternoon shadow after the snow-reflecting sunlight of just minutes earlier. I've never realized how much illumination mountains steal from the valley between them. No wonder Moses—and prophets to follow—sought and found God on a mountain top. *Lux Umbra Dei*: "Light is the Shadow of God."

Yet more revelations lay below. Elisabeth's eyes have been bothering her today, and when I arrive at six in the evening, she suggests that I postpone our conversation until tomorrow. But I am determined not to leave as soon as I've arrived, and so I pointedly leave all the recorders in the bag and offer to do something practical for her, explaining that I have been well trained by both my mother and my wife.

So she has me open a bottle of red wine for her—a "glass and a half"—and as I sip water, we talk over a range of subjects, starting with religion (prompted by her framed photo of our mutual friend Cardinal Schönborn of Vienna).

Elisabeth says she is a great admirer of Cardinal Schönborn, whom I venture may someday be pope. She beams as she declares, "He is very courageous; he says what he thinks." (Obviously a kindred soul).

To her protests that she considers herself "neither Protestant nor Catholic" and "hardly pious," I counter that St. Augustine once said that "whoever sings prays twice." Her singing has surely given more glory to the Creator than a lifetime kneeling in church.

We talk of Strauss's librettist Hugo von Hofmannsthal, whom she considers a great poet. Elisabeth then turns to the framed photograph of her beloved father, "Poppi," and tells me of his lifelong love of books and how his treasured library had been saved in Berlin and shipped to storage in Bavaria toward the end of the war by devoted soldiers who had served under him on the Russian front, where the middle-aged classics teacher had been conscripted to identify the fallen, notify their families back home, and make the arrangements for burial.

By the end of our two-hour talk on and off the record, I ask whether I might go into the music room and play her piano alone—to see whether I might have the nerve to play for her tomorrow. She says yes, but adds she will not promise not to follow me!

And so she does. Sitting by my side, she stops me measure by measure, and offers the most insightful critique and piano lesson I have ever experienced. I should have practiced days if not weeks before coming here. What was I thinking? I sit and wait for the obvious conclusion:

"No wonder you are a writer." Instead, she looks at me with clear blue eyes of wonder and asks, "Why are you not performing?"

To all my excuses—that it was a childhood pursuit, that I don't have the talent, that it is too late, that I don't practice—she counters, "But you must play. Why do you want to write about music when you can make it? You have time to perform—do it!"

I hedge. "I would love to have been able to sing," I say.

"But that is not your instrument. The piano is. Make it sing—and thank God it exists."

Before I flew over here, I wrote to one of my sons that at the risk of sounding morbid, I felt that I was going to Schruns "to meet my fate." I was jesting in earnest. But now it is no joke: life will never be the same. I shall go back to practice, back to musical scores, back to the keyboard of my childhood. Down deep I have always suspected that my musical laziness has taken a toll in true satisfaction, if not happiness. But it took a Dame of the British Empire and a *Kammersängerin* to put it into words—and with blunt, incredulous honesty. Our interview tomorrow will be interesting, to say the least. And I have already promised to return and play again—but after real practice.

I hardly slept at all last night. Was it the cream sauce on the pasta I had for dinner—or something even less easily digested? The realization that a new route has been pointed out for me, and life will never be the same again? I cannot afford to procrastinate or rationalize. Elisabeth speaks with nine decades of experience and a life offered on the altar of music.

As she remarked, music is the only "saint" or holy art permitted in every church of every denomination, from Catholic to the most iconoclastic Protestant one. I shall no longer have the luxury of protesting that I am out of practice—that is no longer an option. As my late Dad put it, "No rush, just do it immediately."

This morning's visit to Elisabeth at eleven was far more relaxed, but it was clear from the start that I would never get her to philosophize about singing or even Mozart's characters. I heard, in the mind's ear, the echo of her Marschallin gently scolding her beloved Oktavian in the early morning light: *"Philosophier' Er nicht, Herr Schatz!"*

She was no philosopher, she protested to me, but "purely practical," and her secrets were reserved only for other singers—of which I am not one. She discounts journalists and critics; hence her conviction that I should exchange my laptop keyboard for a holier one—the piano's!

But then I explained, as I unpacked the recorders, that I was no critic, nor a journalist. In fact, this was my very first interview. She was startled, "Why did you come all this way then?"

"As a pilgrim," I replied—to give thanks to the singer who illuminates my every week, if not day, via recordings. I came purely as a lover of her singing and of Mozart—a listener who still buys her vinyls on eBay to savor the original sound—not as a professional journalist or critic. "This interview," I explained, "was an afterthought with *Opera News*."

"Be sure to tell your readers," she instructed—and so I do.

We moved into the music room and I switched on the recorders for another two hours of discussion. I wanted to learn more about what she termed the "Mozart sound." Even though he wrote Italian operas, it is not an Italian sound, she explained. The Mozart sound remains constant, whether in German or Italian. So how does a young singer find it?

"They have to be taught. You know, sometimes I make students sing a sound thirty times and suddenly on the thirty-first time: 'Ah, that is the sound you are supposed to make.'"

How did she herself find it? Through her teacher Maria Ivogün, and Raucheisen, and later her husband, Walter Legge.

"He had a phenomenal ear and a phenomenal idea of music, not only of Mozart but of all music."

Would she envision the sound in terms of other instruments?

"Not at all—it is enough to have to know your own instrument!"

Yet she would study the full orchestral scores when preparing a role. Violins are key, for they alone can "imitate the vibrato of the human voice." For instance, when singing a passage in which the first violins take the second voice, in accompaniment as though a duet, "you listen to that violin and try to make your voice as similar as you can to that vibrato."

To me, Schwarzkopf made opera singing sound like a chamber music ensemble.

"But of course it is—do you think it could be otherwise? You need to listen closely to the orchestra, to the solo instruments, because the mood of the aria is already set in the introduction, which offers the most revealing notes about the aria, because the aria is but the feeling of what you have said about the situation in the recitative."

"So studying the recitative is no minor matter?"

"Oh, no—it is more important than the aria!"

It was time to approach, gingerly, the heart of the matter: "Why is Mozart the most widely beloved composer? Why not Haydn or Handel, who wrote so many more operas to choose from?"

In three words, "*His melodic instinct*—nonmusicians can leave whistling his melodies."

Schwarzkopf is unusual among singers for her fidelity and devotion to the written texts of the librettists as the inspiration and illumination of the composer's notes. Last night, speaking of Hofmannsthal, whom she considers a great poet, she told me that "everything you need to know about living life is in *Der Rosenkavalier*." So much for the singer who had earlier protested that she had nothing philosophical to say, only the most practical things about the craft of singing!

She remains ever my Marschallin. What opera of Mozart's comes closest to that appraisal of Hofmannsthal?

"*Figaro*, of course."

We took a break as Elisabeth rose from the love seat to take a turn around the room. I offered to try to get her turntable turning again, and play for her the record of *Messiah* highlights, produced by her husband in 1964, his last year at EMI, which I had bought on eBay and brought over to add to her collection.

Her hi-fi was more complicated than any system I have ever confronted, and the large framed photo of Walter Legge did not increase my confidence. But I forged ahead and suggested we listen to "Porgi amor" from the Guilini *Figaro*, my Mozartean grail. It took me awhile to find it, as the record in her library was the Japanese edition ("not legato…good… ja…ok….no…there are things that are really not perfect").

"Would it be interesting," I asked, "to hear the same aria recorded ten years earlier?"

"Yes, cruel but interesting…." I protested that it's surely never cruel to get younger. "Well, I hope it is better."

I put on the 1950 Vienna recording. She was at this point moving from years of Susanna to the Countess; did she still hear the voice of Susanna?

"Yes, all of it…marvelous piano…it's very clean, but it's a child's voice…very sweet…but it's not ripe enough for the countess, much too young."

When I protested that both the Countess and she were indeed young (she was only thirty-four, the Countess perhaps a few years younger), she quipped, "Well, I wasn't eighteen, you know." The Countess is wiser, and should sound "riper," she concluded.

After several more selections, I wore out my welcome with the machinery. "I think you'd better put that energy into piano playing," she laughed.

So I retreated to the piano for a second impromptu coaching session before leaving for the airport. I felt it only fair that I put myself on the receiving end of criticism after inflicting so much audible pain through the poorly tuned loudspeakers. I started with a Bach prelude in C-sharp; the piano itself was sharp, her criticism even sharper—and to the point.

"Could you make it sound like a discussion between the hands? Softer there…discussing…two people discussing, all the time…come in with the left hand…give me those four bars piano…*ta-ta*, quick…two people fighting, discussing."

Then on to Beethoven's "*Ecossaises.*"

"Take an audible breath…can you make that an echo…make that less beautiful…*more*!"

I reminded her that I had taken six trains to reach her; I would not turn back now. Her final prescription was to add more *Fantasie* to the pieces once the technique had been secured. The Haydn sonata, for instance, needed "more visible humor, wit"; the repeats, more color, more variety. The Scarlatti should be turned into a conversation among as many as four people.

Finally, Chopin's "*L'adieu*" waltz.

Can that seem more like a viola coming in there? Start again…Ah! Left hand…You need more freedom…You are not thinking of singing, and you should…even breathing, in and out." It not just about the notes, she stressed. "There are so many possibilities in the music: it's about adding the feelings and human reactions."

I asked whether her performances, even after years of preparation, might change.

"Absolutely, always, in a moment."

She suggested I study some comic actors for the range of human reactions to be translated through the keyboard. Opera without words or *Lieder ohne Worte*. "You should be able to work the piano music into a human expression."

It is, in the end, all a matter of *Fantasie*, her favorite word, of our imagination; not a matter of technical precision—that is just the skeleton (which of course must be sound) on which the flesh and blood interpretation makes a piece of music a living thing. "Music without thoughts, without ideas," she said, "is a waste of time." She claims to be no philosopher, just a "practical singer"—she doth protest too much.

Little did I know what I would take away from this visit, which was initially intended not as an interview but a thank-you for all those years of grace and vocal paradise via recordings. We opened a copy of the new edition of *On and Off the Record*. My favorite photo is one of her looking upward, like a Guido Reni saint in ecstasy—not singing but "listening" (as she inscribed on the verso—"*Hören!*") And that, I concluded, was the key to her success and to her vocal embodiment of the glory of Mozart, *da capo al fine*.

As we said *auf Wiedersehen*—not good-bye—and I promised to practice her lessons before returning in summertime with my wife, she told me to waste no time getting to the keyboard. But which keyboard? Her final question, an encore from last night, gave the answer: "Why do you want to write about music when you can make it?"

I went home by another route. I explained to Elisabeth that I would gladly take six trains to see her, but not to leave her. As I crossed the music room to come around the other side of the loveseat, she turned to me and said, "You know, in this light you seem about seventeen years old!" Then after a pause, she added, "Perhaps part of you still is?" *Ja, ja.* I always loved being a student; it is too late to give it up.

**Postscript**: The first account of this visit was published in the July 2006 issue of *Opera News* under the title "The Voice of Mozart." [The complete text is available on www.charlesscribner.com.] I sent Elisabeth a copy, and held my breath until a phone call from her a week later: she told me that of all the profiles written of her over the years, it was her favorite. That was the last time I spoke with her; two weeks later she died in her sleep.

*"Die Zeit, die ist ein sonderbar Ding…Auch sie ist ein Geschöpf des Vaters der uns alle erschaffen hat."* Time is a strange thing…yet it too is a creation of the Father who made us all.

**In Memoriam**: *Dame Elisabeth Schwarzkopf (1915–2006)*